# The GIFT

## ALSO BY EDITH EGER

*The Choice*

# EDITH EGER

# The GIFT

A survivor's journey to freedom

**RIDER**

2

Rider, an imprint of Ebury Publishing,
20 Vauxhall Bridge Road,
London SW1V 2SA

Rider is part of the Penguin Random House group of companies
whose addresses can be found at global.penguinrandomhouse.com

Penguin
Random House
UK

First published in Great Britain by Rider in 2020
This edition published in 2021
Published in the United States by Scribner, an imprint of Simon & Schuster, Inc.
1230 Avenue of the Americas, New York, NY 10020

www.penguin.co.uk

A CIP catalogue record for this book is available from the British Library

ISBN 9781846046285

Printed and bound in India by Thomson Press India Ltd.
The authorised representative in the EEA is Penguin Random House Ireland,
Morrison Chambers, 32 Nassau Street, Dublin D02 YH68.

MIX
Paper from
responsible sources
FSC® C018179

*To my patients. You are my teachers. You gave me the courage to return to Auschwitz and to begin my journey toward forgiveness and freedom. You continue to inspire me through your honesty and courage.*

# CONTENTS

# INTRODUCTION

# Unlocking our Mental Prisons

# *I learned how to live at a death camp*

In the spring of 1944, I was sixteen, living with my parents and two older sisters in Kassa, Hungary. There were signs of war and prejudice all around us. The yellow stars we wore pinned to our coats. The Hungarian Nazis—*nyilas*—who occupied our old apartment. Newspaper accounts of battlefronts and German occupation spreading across Europe. The worried glances my parents exchanged at the table. The awful day when I was cut from the Olympic gymnastics team because I was Jewish. Yet I had been blissfully preoccupied with ordinary teenage concerns. I was in love with my first boyfriend, Eric, the tall, intelligent boy I'd met in book club. I replayed our first kiss and admired the new blue silk dress that my father had designed for me. I marked my progress in the ballet and gymnastics studio, and joked with Magda, my beautiful eldest sister, and Klara, who was studying violin at a conservatory in Budapest.

3

And then everything changed.

One cold dawn in April the Jews of Kassa were rounded up and imprisoned in an old brick factory at the edge of town. A few weeks later, Magda and my parents and I were loaded into a cattle car bound for Auschwitz. My parents were murdered in the gas chambers the day we arrived.

My first night in Auschwitz, I was forced to dance for SS officer Josef Mengele, known as the Angel of Death, the man who had scrutinized the new arrivals as we came through the selection line that day and sent my mother to her death. "Dance for me!" he ordered, and I stood on the cold concrete floor of the barracks, frozen with fear. Outside, the camp orchestra began to play a waltz, "The Blue Danube." Remembering my mother's advice—*No one can take from you what you've put in your mind*—I closed my eyes and retreated to an inner world. In my mind, I was no longer imprisoned in a death camp, cold and hungry and ruptured by loss. I was on the stage of the Budapest opera house, dancing the role of Juliet in Tchaikovsky's ballet. From within this private refuge I willed my arms to lift and my legs to twirl. I summoned the strength to dance for my life.

Each moment in Auschwitz was hell on earth. It was also my best classroom. Subjected to loss, torture, starvation, and the constant threat of death, I discovered the tools for survival and freedom that I continue to use every day in my clinical psychology practice as well as in my own life.

As I write this introduction in the fall of 2019, I am ninety-two. I earned my doctorate in clinical psychology in 1978 and I've been treating patients in a therapeutic setting for over forty years. I have worked with combat veterans and survivors of sexual assault; students, civic leaders, and CEOs; people battling addiction and those struggling with anxiety and depression; couples grappling with resentment and those longing to rekindle intimacy; parents and children learning how to live together and those discovering how to live apart. As a psychologist; as a mother, grandmother, and great-grandmother; as an observer of my own and others' behavior; and as an Auschwitz survivor, I am here to tell you that the worst prison is not the one the Nazis put me in. The worst prison is the one I built for myself.

Although our lives have probably been very different, perhaps you know what I mean. Many of us experience feeling trapped in our minds. Our thoughts and beliefs determine, and often limit, how we feel, what we do, and what we think is possible. In my work I've discovered that while our imprisoning beliefs show up and play out in unique ways, there are some common mental prisons that contribute to suffering. This book is a practical guide to help us identify our mental prisons and develop the tools we need to become free.

The foundation of freedom is the power to choose. In the final months of the war, I had very few options, and no way to escape. Hungarian Jews had been among the last in Europe to be deported to death camps, and after eight months in Auschwitz, just before the Russian army defeated Germany, my sister and I and a hundred other prisoners were evacuated from Auschwitz and marched from Poland, through Germany, to Austria. We performed slave labor in factories along the way, and rode on top of trains transporting German ammunition, our bodies used as human shields to protect the cargo from British bombs. (The British bombed the trains anyway.)

When my sister and I were liberated at Gunskirchen—a concentration camp in Austria—in May 1945, a little over a year after we'd been taken prisoner, my parents and almost all the people I knew were dead. My back had broken from constant physical abuse. I was starving, covered in sores, and could barely move from where I lay in a pile of corpses; people who had been sick and starving like me, whose bodies had given up. I couldn't undo what had been done to me. I couldn't control how many people the Nazis had shoved into the cattle cars or crematoria, trying to exterminate as many Jews and "undesirables" as they could before the end of the war. I couldn't alter the systematic dehumanization or slaughter of the over six million innocents who died in the camps. All I could do was decide how to respond to terror and hopelessness. Somehow, I found it within myself to choose hope.

But surviving Auschwitz was only the first leg of my journey to freedom. For many decades, I remained a prisoner of the past. On the surface, I was doing well, putting my trauma behind me and moving on. I married Béla, the son of a prominent family in Prešov who had been a partisan during the war, fighting the Nazis in the mountain forests of Slovakia. I became a mother, fled the Communists in Europe, immigrated to America, lived on pennies, rose out of poverty, and, in my forties, went to college. I became a high school teacher, and then returned to school for a master's in educational psychology and a doctorate in clinical psychology. Even late in my graduate training, committed to helping others heal and trusted with some of the toughest cases during my clinical rotations, I was still in hiding—running from the past, denying my grief and trauma, minimizing and pretending, trying to please others and do things perfectly, blaming Béla for my chronic resentment and disappointment, chasing after achievement as though it could make up for all I'd lost.

One day I arrived at the William Beaumont Army Medical Center at Fort Bliss, Texas, where I held a competitive clinical internship, and put on my white coat and name tag: Dr. Eger, Department of Psychiatry. But for a split second the words blurred and it seemed to say, Dr. Eger, Impostor. That's when I knew I couldn't support others in healing if I didn't heal myself.

My therapeutic approach is eclectic and intuitive, a blend of insight- and cognitive-oriented theories and practices. I call it choice therapy, as freedom is fundamentally about choice. While suffering is inevitable and universal, we can always choose how we respond, and I seek to highlight and harness my patients' power to choose—to effect positive change in their lives.

My work is rooted in four core psychological principles:

First, from Martin Seligman and positive psychology, the concept of "learned helplessness"—that we suffer most when we believe that we have no efficacy in our lives, that nothing we do can improve the outcome. We flourish when we harness "learned optimism"—the strength, resiliency, and ability to create the meaning and direction of our lives.

Second, from cognitive-behavioral therapy, the understanding that our thoughts create our feelings and behavior. To change harmful, dysfunctional, or self-defeating behaviors, we change our thoughts; we replace our negative beliefs with those that serve and support our growth.

Third, from Carl Rogers, one of my most influential mentors, the importance of unconditional positive self-regard. Much of our suffering stems from our misconception that we can't be loved *and* genuine—that if we are to earn others' acceptance and approval, we must deny or hide our true selves. In my work I strive to extend unconditional love to my patients, and to guide them to discover that we become free when we stop wearing masks and fulfilling the roles and expectations others assign us, and start unconditionally loving ourselves.

Finally, I work from the understanding, shared with my beloved mentor, friend, and fellow Auschwitz survivor Viktor Frankl, that our worst experiences can be our best teachers, catalyzing unforeseen discoveries and opening us up to new possibilities and perspectives. Healing, fulfillment, and freedom come from our ability to choose our response to whatever life brings us, and to make meaning and derive purpose from all we experience—and in particular, from our suffering.

Freedom is a lifetime practice—a choice we get to make again and again each day. Ultimately, freedom requires hope, which I define in two ways: the awareness that suffering, however terrible, is temporary; and the curiosity to discover *what happens next*. Hope allows us to live in the present instead of the past, and to unlock the doors of our mental prisons.

Three-quarters of a century after liberation, I still have nightmares. I suffer flashbacks. Till the day I die, I will grieve the loss of my parents, who never got to see four generations rise from the ashes of their deaths. The horror is still with me. There's no freedom in minimizing what happened, or in trying to forget.

But remembering and honoring are very different from remaining stuck in guilt, shame, anger, resentment, or fear about the past. I can face the reality of what happened and remember that although I have lost, I've never stopped choosing love and hope. For me, the ability to choose, even in the midst of so much suffering and powerlessness, is the true gift that came out of my time in Auschwitz.

It may seem wrong to call anything that came out of the death camps a gift. How could anything good come from hell? The constant fear that I'd be pulled out of the selection line or the barrack at any moment and thrown in the gas chamber, the dark smoke rising from the chimneys, a pervasive reminder of all I'd lost and stood to lose. I had no control over the senseless, excruciating circumstances. But I could focus on what I held in my mind. I could respond, not react. Auschwitz provided the opportunity to discover my inner strength and my power of choice. I learned to rely on parts of myself I would otherwise never have known were there.

We all have this capacity to choose. When nothing helpful or nourishing is coming from the outside, that is precisely the moment when we have the possibility to discover who we really are. It's not what happens to us that matters most, it's what we do with our experiences.

When we escape our mental prisons, we not only become free *from* what has held us back, but free *to* exercise our own free will. I first learned the difference between negative and positive freedom on liberation day at Gunskirchen in May 1945 when I was seventeen. I was lying on the muddy ground in a pile of the dead and dying when the Seventy-First Infantry arrived to free the camp. I remember the soldiers' eyes full of shock, bandanas tied over their faces to block out the stench of rotting flesh. In those first hours of freedom, I watched my fellow former prisoners—

those who were capable of walking—leave through the prison gates. Moments later, they returned and sat listlessly on the damp grass or on the dirt floors of the barracks, unable to move forward. Viktor Frankl noted the same phenomenon when Soviet forces liberated Auschwitz. We were no longer in prison, but many of us weren't yet able, physically or mentally, to recognize our freedom. We were so eroded by disease, starvation, and trauma, we had no capacity to take responsibility for our lives. We could hardly remember how to be ourselves.

We'd finally been released *from* the Nazis. But we weren't yet free.

I now recognize that the most damaging prison is in our mind, and the key is in our pocket. No matter how great our suffering or how strong the bars, it's possible to break free from whatever's holding us back.

It is not easy. But it is so worth it.

In *The Choice*, I told the story of my journey from imprisonment to liberation and then on to true freedom. I've been astounded and humbled by the book's global reception and by all the readers who shared stories of how they have confronted their own pasts and worked to heal their pain. We were able to connect, sometimes in person, sometimes through email, social media, or video calls, and many of the stories I heard are included in this book. (Names and other identifying details have been changed to protect privacy.)

As I wrote in *The Choice*, I don't want people to read my story and think, "There's no way my suffering compares to hers." I want people to hear my story and think, "If she can do it, so can

I!" Many have asked for a practical guide to the healing I've done in my own life and with my patients in my clinical work. *The Gift* is that book.

In each chapter, I explore a common prison of the mind, illustrating its effects and challenges with stories from my life and clinical work, and closing with keys to free ourselves from that mental prison. Some of the keys are questions that could be used as journal prompts or in discussion with a trusted friend or therapist; others are actionable steps you can take right now to improve your life and relationships. Though healing is not a linear process, I've organized the chapters in an intentional sequence that reflects the arc of my own journey toward freedom. That said, the chapters can also stand alone or be read in any order. You're the director of your own journey; I invite you to use the book in whatever way best serves you.

And I offer three initial guideposts to start you on the path to freedom.

We do not change until we're ready. Sometimes it's a tough circumstance—perhaps a divorce, accident, illness, or death— that forces us to face up to what isn't working and try something else. Sometimes our inner pain or unfulfilled longing gets so loud and insistent that we can't ignore it another minute. But readiness doesn't come from the outside, and it can't be rushed or forced. You're ready when you're ready, when something inside shifts and you decide, *Until now I did that. Now I'm going to do something else.*

**WE DO NOT CHANGE UNTIL WE'RE READY.**

Change is about interrupting the habits and patterns that no longer serve us. If you want to meaningfully alter your life, you

> **CHANGE IS ABOUT INTERRUPTING THE HABITS AND PATTERNS THAT NO LONGER SERVE US.**

don't simply abandon a dysfunctional habit or belief; you replace it with a healthy one. You choose what you're moving toward. You find an arrow and follow it. As you begin your journey, it's important to reflect not only on what you'd like to be free *from*, but on what you want to be free *to* do or become.

Finally, when you change your life, it isn't to become the *new* you. It's to become the *real* you—the one-of-a-kind diamond

> **WHEN YOU CHANGE YOUR LIFE, IT'S TO BECOME THE *REAL* YOU.**

that will never exist again and can never be replaced. Everything that's happened to you— all the choices you've made until now, all the ways you've tried to cope—it all matters; it's all useful. You don't have to throw everything out and start from scratch. Whatever you've done, it's brought you this far, to this moment.

The ultimate key to freedom is to keep becoming who you truly are.

# CHAPTER 1

# What Now?

## The Prison of Victimhood

In my experience, victims ask, "Why me?" Survivors ask, "What now?"

Suffering is universal. But victimhood is optional. There is no way to escape being hurt or oppressed by other people or circumstances. The only guarantee is that no matter how kind we are or how hard we work, we're going to have pain. We're going to be affected by environmental and genetic factors over which we have little or no control. But we each get to choose whether or not we stay a victim. We don't get to choose what happens to us, but we do get to choose how we respond to our experience.

Many of us stay in a prison of victimhood because, subconsciously, it feels safer. We ask "Why?" over and over, believing that if we could just figure out the reason, the pain would lessen. Why did I get cancer? Why did I lose my job? Why did my partner have an affair? We search for answers, for understanding, as if there's a logical reason to explain why things happened the way they did. But when we ask why, we're stuck searching for someone or something to blame—including ourselves.

Why did this happen to me?

Well, why *not* you?

Maybe I went to Auschwitz and survived so I could talk to you now, so I could live as an example of how to be a survivor instead of a victim. When I ask "What now?" instead of "Why me?" I stop focusing on why this bad thing happened—or is happening—and start paying attention to what I can do with my experience. I'm not looking for a savior or a scapegoat. Instead, I begin to look at choices and at possibilities.

My parents didn't have a choice in how their lives ended. But I have many choices. I can feel guilty that I survived when so many millions, including my mother and father, perished. Or I can choose to live and work and heal in a way that releases the hold of the past. I can embrace my strength and freedom.

Victimhood is rigor mortis of the mind. It's stuck in the past, stuck in the pain, and stuck on the losses and deficits: *what I can't do* and *what I don't have*.

This is the first tool for moving out of victimhood: approach whatever is happening with a gentle embrace. It doesn't mean you have to like what's happening. But when you stop fighting and resisting, you have more energy and imagination at the ready to figure out "What now?" To move forward instead of nowhere. To discover what you want and need in this moment, and where you want to go from here.

Every behavior satisfies a need. Many of us choose to stay victims because it gives us license to do zero on our own behalf. Freedom comes with a price. We're called to be accountable for our own behavior—and to take responsibility even in situations we didn't cause or choose.

Life is full of surprises.

A few weeks before Christmas, Emily—forty-five, mother of two, happily married for eleven years—sat down with her husband after the children had gone to bed. She was about to suggest they watch a movie when he looked at her and calmly said the words that would upend her life.

"I met someone," he said. "We're in love. I don't think you and I should be married anymore."

Emily was completely floored. She couldn't see a way forward. And then the next surprise came. She had breast cancer; a large tumor that required immediate, aggressive chemotherapy. During the first weeks of treatment, she felt paralyzed. Her husband postponed discussion about the state of their marriage to see her through the months of chemo, but Emily was in a daze.

"I thought my whole life had come to an end," she said. "I thought I was a dying woman."

But when I spoke to her eight months after her diagnosis, she'd just had surgery and received more unexpected news: she'd achieved complete remission.

"The doctors never would have predicted it," she said. "It's really a miracle."

Her cancer is gone. But so is her husband. After her chemo ended, he told her he'd made his decision. He'd rented an apartment. He wanted a divorce.

"I was so frightened to die," Emily told me. "Now I have to learn to live."

She's consumed by worry for her children, by the hurt of betrayal, concerns over finances, and loneliness, so vast it's like she's fallen off the edge of a cliff.

"I'm still finding it so hard to say yes to my life," she said.

The divorce has thrown her into her worst fear made real, a deep-seated terror of abandonment she's harbored since she was four, when her mother became clinically depressed. Her dad turned silent about her mom's illness, escaping into work, leaving Emily to make it on her own. When her mother later died by suicide, it confirmed the reality she knew yet sought to avoid: that the people you love disappear.

"I've always been in a relationship, since I was fifteen," she said. "I never learned to be happy on my own, with myself, to love myself." Her voice breaks when she says those words: *love myself*.

I often say that we need to give our children roots, and give them wings. We need to do the same for ourselves. The only one you have is you. You're born alone. You die alone. So start by getting up in the morning and going to the mirror. Look yourself in the eye and say, "I love you." Say, "I'm never going to leave you." Hug yourself. Kiss yourself. Try it!

And then keep showing up for yourself all day, every day.

"But how do I deal with my husband?" Emily asked. "When we meet, he seems totally calm and relaxed. He's happy with his decision. But all my emotions come out. I start crying. I can't control myself when I see him."

"You can if you want to," I told her. "But you have to want to, and I can't make you want to. I don't have that power. You do.

Make a decision. You may feel like screaming and crying. But don't act on it unless it's in your best interest."

Sometimes it just takes one sentence to point the way out of victimhood: *Is it good for me?*

Is it good for me to sleep with a married man? Is it good for me to eat a piece of chocolate cake? Is it good for me to beat my cheating husband on the chest with my fist? Is it good for me to go dancing? To help a friend? Does it deplete me or empower me?

Another tool for moving out of victimhood is to learn to cope with loneliness. It's what most of us fear more than anything else. But when you're in love with yourself, alone doesn't mean lonely.

"Loving yourself is good for your kids, too," I told Emily. "When you show them that you'll never lose you, you show them that they're not losing you, either. That you're here now. Then they can live their lives, rather than you worrying about them, and them worrying about you, and everybody worrying, worrying. To your children, and to yourself, you say, 'I'm here. I'm showing up for you.' You'll give them—and yourself—what you never had: a healthy mother."

When we start loving ourselves, we start patching up the holes in our hearts, the gaping places that feel like they'll never be filled. And we start making discoveries. "Aha!" we learn to say. "I didn't see it that way before." I asked Emily what discoveries she'd made in the last eight months of turmoil. Her eyes brightened.

"I've discovered how many wonderful people I have around me—my family, friends, people I didn't know before who became friends during my therapy. When the doctor told me I had cancer, I thought my life had come to an end. Now I've met so many people. I've learned I can fight, that I'm powerful. It took me forty-five years to learn that, but I'm lucky I know it now. My new life is already beginning."

We can all find strength and freedom, even within terrible circumstances. Honey, you're in charge, so take charge. Don't be Cinderella, sitting in the kitchen waiting for a guy with a foot fetish. There are no princes or princesses. You have all the love and power you need within. So write down what you want to achieve, the kind of life you want to live, the kind of partner you want to have. When you go out, look like a million-dollar baby. Join a group of people dealing with similar struggles, where you can care for each other and commit yourselves to something bigger than yourselves. And then get curious. What's next? How's it going to turn out?

Our minds come up with all sorts of brilliant ways to protect us. Victimhood is a tempting shield because it suggests that if we make ourselves blameless, our grief will hurt less. As long as Emily identified as the victim, she could pass all the blame and responsibility for her well-being on to her ex-husband. Victimhood offers a false respite by deferring and delaying growth. The longer we stay there, the harder it is to leave.

"You're not a victim," I told Emily. "It's not who you are—it's what was done to you."

We can be wounded *and* accountable. Responsible *and* innocent. We can give up the secondary gains of victimhood for the primary gains of growing and healing and moving on.

The whole reason to step out of victimhood is so we can step into the rest of our lives. Barbara was trying to navigate this pivot when she contacted me a year after her mother's death. She looked young for sixty-four, her skin smooth, highlights in her long blond hair. But she seemed to hold a heavy burden in her chest, and her wide blue eyes were full of sorrow.

Barbara's relationship with her mother had been complicated, and so her grief was also complicated. Demanding and controlling, her mother had sometimes explicitly reinforced Barbara's victimhood, fixating on problems like bad grades and breakups, stoking Barbara's belief that she was flawed and helpless and would never amount to much. In some ways, it was a relief to be free from her mother's distorted and critical perspective. But she also felt restless and unsettled. A recent back injury had interrupted the job she loved at a local café, and she had trouble falling asleep at night, her mind churning with questions. *Is my time almost up? What have I failed at? What have I done to be remembered? What is the outcome of my life?*

**THE WHOLE REASON TO STEP OUT OF VICTIMHOOD IS SO WE CAN STEP INTO THE REST OF OUR LIVES.**

"I feel sad and anxious and insecure," she said. "I just can't come to any peace."

I often see this happen to middle-aged women who have lost their mothers. The unfinished emotional business of the relationship lives on—and death makes it feel impossible that there will ever be closure.

"Have you released your mom from the past?" I asked.

Barbara shook her head. Her eyes filled with tears.

Tears are good. They mean we've been pierced by an important emotional truth. If I ask a question that prompts a patient to cry, it's like striking gold. We've hit on something essential. Yet the moment of release is as vulnerable as it is profound. I leaned in, all present, no rush.

Barbara wiped her face and took a long, shaky breath. "I want to ask you about something," she said. "A memory from childhood I keep replaying nonstop in my mind."

I asked her to close her eyes while she described the incident, to tell it in present tense, as though it were happening now.

"I'm three," she began. "We're all in the kitchen. My dad's at the breakfast table. My mom is standing over me and my older brother. She's angry. She lines us up side by side and says, 'Who do you like best, me or your father?' My dad is watching it happen, and he starts to cry. He says, 'Don't do that. Don't do that to the kids.' I want to say that I love my dad best; I want to go over and sit in his lap and hug him. But I can't do that. I can't say that I love him or I'll make my mom mad. I'll get in trouble. So I say I like my mom the best. And now . . ." Her voice cracked, tears rolling down her cheeks. "Now I wish I could take it back."

"You were a good survivor," I told her. "A smart cookie. You did what you had to do to survive."

"Then why does it hurt so much?" she said. "Why can't I just let it go?"

"Because that little girl doesn't know she's safe now. Take me to her there in the kitchen," I said. "Tell me what you see."

She described the window facing the backyard, the yellow flowers on the handles of the cabinet doors, how her eyes were exactly the height of the oven dials.

"Talk to that little girl. How is she feeling now?"

"I love my dad. But I can't say it."

"You're powerless."

Tears spilled down her cheeks to her chin. She wiped at them, then cradled her face in her hands.

"You were a child then," I said. "You're an adult now. Go to that precious, one-of-a-kind little girl. Be her mother now. Take her hand and tell her, 'I'm going to take you out of here.'"

Barbara's eyes were still closed. She swayed side to side.

"Hold her hand," I continued. "Walk her to the door, down the front steps, out to the sidewalk. Walk her up the block. Turn the corner. Tell the little girl, 'You're not stuck there anymore.'"

The prison of victimhood often gets established in childhood, and even when we're adults, it can keep us feeling as powerless as we did when we were young. We can release ourselves from victimhood by helping that inner child feel safe, and by letting her experience the world with an adult's autonomy.

I guided Barbara to keep holding the hand of the wounded little girl. To take her for a walk. Show her the flowers in the park. Spoil her and love her right up. Give her an ice cream cone or a soft teddy bear to squeeze—whatever she wanted most to feel safe. "And then take her down to the beach," I said. "Show her how to kick the sand. Tell her, 'I'm here and we're going to be angry.' Kick the sand with her. Yell and shout. Then take her home. Not back to the kitchen, but where you live now. The place where you'll always show up to take care of her."

Barbara's eyes were still closed, her mouth and cheeks more relaxed. But a furrow of tension still gathered between her eyes.

"That little girl was stuck in the kitchen, and she needed you to get her out," I said. "You rescued her."

She nodded slowly, but the tension didn't leave her face.

Her work in the kitchen wasn't done. There were others to rescue.

"Your mother needs you, too," I said. "She's still standing in that kitchen. Open the door for her. Tell her it's time for both of you to be free."

Barbara imagined going to her father first, to the breakfast table where he still sat in silence, his cheeks wet with tears. She kissed him on the forehead and spoke the love she'd had to hide as a child. Then she went to her mother. She put a hand on her shoulder, looked into her troubled eyes, and nodded toward the open door, the patch of green lawn visible from where they stood. When Barbara opened her eyes, something in her face and shoulders appeared to relax.

"Thank you," she said.

Releasing ourselves from victimhood also means releasing others from the roles we've assigned them.

I had a chance to use this tool myself a few months ago, when I was on a speaking tour in Europe and invited my daughter Audrey to go with me. When she'd been in middle school and high school, training as a Junior Olympic swimmer, getting up at five in the morning for practice, her hair green from the constant exposure to chlorine, her father had usually been the one to accompany her to swim meets all over Texas and the Southwest. This was how Béla and I had managed the demands of our careers and three children—we'd acted as partners, splitting responsibilities. But that meant we each missed out on things. Traveling with Audrey now couldn't replace the time we'd lost when she was younger. But it seemed like a welcome way to honor our relationship. Besides, this time I was the one who needed a chaperone!

We went to the Netherlands, and then on to Switzerland,

where we sank our teeth into napoleon pastries as rich and sweet as the ones my father used to sneak home for me at night when he'd been out playing billiards. I'd been back to Europe numerous times since the war, but it was incredibly healing for me to be there, so close to my childhood and my trauma, with my magnificent daughter, to share silence and conversation, to hear her plans for launching a second career as a grief and leadership coach. One night, after I gave a speech to a roomful of global executives at a business school in Lausanne, someone surprised me by asking, "What's it like, traveling with Audrey?"

I searched for the words to adequately convey how special this time was to me. I mentioned that middle children often get short shrift in families, and that Audrey had been raised largely by her older sister, Marianne, while I was running their little brother, John, all over El Paso—and even as far as Baltimore—in search of therapies for some undiagnosed developmental delays of great concern. John went on to graduate from the University of Texas as one of the top ten students in his class, and is now a respected civic leader and advocate for people with disabilities. I'm forever grateful he was able to receive interventions and vital support. But I've always felt guilty for the ways John's unique needs occupied my attention and interrupted Audrey's childhood, for the six-year age gap between Marianne and Audrey, for the burden my own trauma put on my children. Saying this impromptu, in public, was cathartic for me. It felt good to recognize it, to apologize.

But at the airport the next morning, Audrey confronted me.

"Mom," she said, "we have to change the story of who I am. I don't see myself as a victim. I need you to stop seeing me that way."

My chest tightened with discomfort, with the rush to defend

myself. I thought I'd been portraying her as a survivor, not a victim. But she was absolutely right. In trying to discharge my own guilt, I'd cast her in the role of the neglected child. I'd put us all in roles: I was the victimizer, Audrey the victim, and Marianne the rescuer. (Or, in another version of the same story, I cast John as the victim, myself as the rescuer, and Béla, whom I was so angry with in those years, as the victimizer.) The role of victim is often passed back and forth in relationships and families. But there can't be a victim without a victimizer. When we stay a victim, or put someone else in that role, we reinforce and perpetuate the harm. In focusing on what Audrey *hadn't* had growing up, I was undermining her survivor strength—her capacity to see any experience as an opportunity for growth. And I was trapping myself in a prison of guilt.

The first time I saw the power of the perspective shift from victim to survivor in action was as a clinical intern at the William Beaumont Army Medical Center, in the mid-1970s. One day I was assigned two new patients, both Vietnam veterans, both paraplegics with injuries of the lower spinal cord, both unlikely to walk again. They had the same diagnosis, the same prognosis. The first spent hours curled up in the fetal position on his bed, full of rage, cursing God and country. The other preferred to be out of bed, sitting up in his wheelchair. "I'm seeing everything differently now," he told me. "My children came to visit me yesterday, and now that I'm in this wheelchair, I'm so much closer to their eyes." He wasn't happy to be disabled, to have compromised sexual function, to wonder if he'd ever be able to run a race with his daughter or dance at his son's wedding. But he could see that his injury had afforded him a new perspective. And he could choose to see his injury as limiting and incapacitating—or as a new source of growth.

More than forty years later, in the spring of 2018, I saw my daughter Marianne make a similar choice. While traveling in Italy with her husband, Rob, she tripped on a set of stone steps and fell on her head, suffering a traumatic brain injury. For two weeks, we didn't know if she would survive. Or, if she survived, who she would be. Would she be able to speak? Would she remember her children, her three beautiful grandsons, Rob, her siblings, me? Throughout those insufferable days when her life hung in the balance, I reached again and again to touch the bracelet Béla gave me when she was born, a thick braid made from three kinds of gold. When we'd fled Czechoslovakia in 1949, I smuggled it out in Marianne's diaper. I've worn it every day since, a talisman of the life and love that emerge even from destruction and death, a reminder that there's such a thing as survival against the odds.

For me, there is no more difficult feeling than fear mixed with powerlessness. I was gutted by Marianne's suffering, terrified that we'd lose her—and there was nothing concrete to *do* about it, to heal her, to prevent the worst from happening. The fear would rise, and I'd say her Hungarian nickname, "Marchuka, Marchuka," the syllables a kind of prayer. I realized it's what I'd done in Auschwitz when I danced for Josef Mengele. Gone inward. Created a sanctuary inside myself, a place to keep my spirit safe within the turmoil of threat and uncertainty.

Miraculously, Marianne survived. She doesn't remember the first weeks after the fall. Perhaps she went inward, too. Somehow—through excellent medical care, the constant support and presence of her husband and family, her own inner resources—she was able, bit by bit, to regain physical and cognitive function, to remember her children's names. At first, it was difficult for her to swallow, and her sense of taste was distorted. I cooked for her nonstop, determined to try all of the foods she used to love. One day she asked me to make trepanka, a potato dish served with sauerkraut and brinza, a Czech farmer's cheese. It was the food I most craved when I was pregnant with her! When I watched her try a first bite and smile, I felt deep in my bones that she was going to be okay.

In just a year and a half, she's made a stunning recovery and is living and working as she did before the injury, with strength, brilliance, creativity, and passion.

Though many aspects of her recovery are out of her control, not easily explained, a matter of sheer luck, she's also made choices that I know have helped her heal. When you're in a vulnerable position, with limited energy, it is especially crucial to choose how to spend your time. Marianne has chosen to think like a survivor, focusing on what she needs to do to keep improving, listening to her body to know when it's time to rest, and feeling and expressing gratitude for her health and all the people who are supporting her recovery. When she wakes up in the morning, she asks herself, "What am I going to do today? When will I do my therapy exercises? What projects do I want to work on? What do I need to do to take care of myself?"

Attitude isn't everything. We can't erase hardships or make ourselves well with our outlook alone. But how we spend our time and mental energy does affect our health. If we resist and rail against what we're experiencing, we take away from our growth and healing. Instead, we can acknowledge the awful thing that is happening *and* find the best way to live with it.

This is especially true when we come up against setbacks or

complications in our healing process. Brain injuries generally mean that patients are not as good at many of the things they used to do with ease or skill. Marianne is still working hard to reestablish all the neural networks that were damaged by the fall. She tires easily with too much standing or walking, and struggles with language retrieval. Except for the initial weeks of recovery, her memories are intact, but sometimes she can't find the words for things—the name of a country she's visited or a vegetable she wants to buy at the farmers market. She's had to learn new methods for doing what she used to do effortlessly. When she prepares for a speech, she can't just write down three points and trust her brain to remember the connections and fill in the gaps, as she did before her injury. Now she has to write down the entire speech—every word, every transition.

But interestingly, there are other things she does with more flexibility and innovation. She's always been an accomplished home chef, and once had a cooking column in a San Diego newspaper. After her fall, she has had to reteach herself how to cook. In the process, she has begun inventing new recipes and going about old processes in a new way. She and Rob live in Manhattan now, but they spend as much of the summer as they can in La Jolla, where I live. This past summer she wanted to make me a cold cherry soup she'd prepared once for a dinner party in New York. She bought a bunch of sour cherries and reread two old Hungarian cookbooks, only to abandon the cookbooks and go about it her own way—preparing the soup cold instead of heating it and then cooling it down, adding three different kinds of fruit. Without the constant adaptations she's had to make since the injury, she probably would have made the soup the same way she had before. Instead, she embraced the practice of reinvention her injury has required and let it guide her to something new. And it was delicious!

I can see in her eyes sometimes how tiring and frustrating it is to work so hard to do things she once took for granted. But she's also attuned to the possibilities.

"It's funny," she told me, "but I feel like I'm intellectually alive in a different way." Her face lit up the way it had as a child when she'd learned to read. "To tell you the truth, it's kind of fun and thrilling."

This isn't an uncommon experience for people who've survived similar injuries. Marianne's neurologist told her a number of his patients, never skilled artists, suddenly found after a major brain injury that they could draw or paint—and do it remarkably well. Something about the broken and reconfigured neural pathways allows many survivors to find they're in possession of gifts they never had or knew about before.

**IN EVERY CRISIS THERE IS A TRANSITION.**

What a beautiful reminder that the things that interrupt our lives, that stop us in our tracks, can also be catalysts for the emerging self, tools that show us a new way to be, that endow us with new vision.

This is why I say that in every crisis there is a transition. Awful things happen, and they hurt like hell. And these devastating experiences are also opportunities to regroup and decide what we want for our lives. When we choose to respond to what's happened by moving forward and discovering our freedom *to*, we release ourselves from the prison of victimhood.

# KEYS TO FREE YOURSELF FROM VICTIMHOOD

- *That was then, this is now.* Think of a moment in childhood or adolescence when you felt hurt by another's actions, large or small. Try to think of a specific moment, not a generalized impression of that relationship or time of life. Imagine the moment as though you are reliving it. Pay attention to sensory details—sights, sounds, smells, tastes, physical sensations. Then picture yourself as you are now. See yourself enter the past moment and take your past self by the hand. Guide yourself out of the place where you were hurt, out of the past. Tell yourself, "Here I am. I'm going to take care of you."

- *In every crisis there is a transition.* Write a letter to a person or situation that has caused you pain, recently or in the past. Be specific about what the person did, or about what happened that you didn't like. Put it all on the table. Say how the actions, words, or events affected you. Then write another letter to the same person or situation—but this time write a thank-you letter, expressing gratitude for what the person has taught you about yourself or how the situation has prompted you to grow. The goal of the thank-you letter is not to pretend to like something you didn't like, or to force yourself to be happy about something painful. Acknowledge that what happened wasn't right and that it hurt. And also notice the healing power in shifting your point of view from a powerless victim to who you really are: a survivor, a person of strength.

- *Harness your freedom to.* *Make a vision board—a visual representation of what you want to create or embrace in your life. Cut out pictures and words from magazines, old calendars, etc.—there are no rules, just see what attracts you. Paste the images and words to a sheet of poster board or a big piece of cardboard. Notice what patterns emerge. (This is a wonderful practice to do together with dear friends—and with plenty of good food!) Keep your vision board close by and look at it every day. Let this intuitive creation be an arrow to follow.*

# CHAPTER 2

# No Prozac
at Auschwitz

## The Prison of Avoidance

One day when Marianne was five and we were living in a tiny apartment in Baltimore, she came home from school crying. She hadn't been invited to a birthday party, and her heart was crushed, her face red with emotion, her cheeks covered in tears. I didn't know anything about how to be present with feelings. I didn't know how to let her have her own feelings. In those days, I was in complete denial about my past. I never spoke of Auschwitz. Even my own children wouldn't know I was a survivor until Marianne was in middle school and found a book about the Holocaust. When she showed her father the pictures of starving, skeletal people in Auschwitz and demanded to know what terrible calamity had people dying behind barbed wire, it broke my heart to listen as he told her I'd been a prisoner there. I hid in the bathroom, unsure how to meet my daughter's eyes.

When Marianne came home from kindergarten in tears, her sadness made me sad and uncomfortable. So I led her by the hand into the kitchen and made her a chocolate milkshake. I served her a big piece of Hungarian seven-layer chocolate cake. That was my remedy—eat something sweet. Cure your discomfort with food. Food was my answer to everything. (Especially chocolate. And especially Hungarian chocolate, with unsalted butter. Don't ever put salt in the butter and make a Hungarian anything!)

I didn't know it then, but we disable our children when we take away their suffering. We teach them that feelings are wrong or scary. But a feeling is only a feeling. There's no right or wrong. There's just my feeling and yours. We are wiser not to try to reason others out of their feelings, or try to cheer them up. It's better to allow their feelings and keep them company, to say, "Tell me more." To resist saying what I used to tell my children when they were upset because someone had teased or excluded them: "I know how you feel." It's a lie. You can't ever know how someone else feels. It's not happening to you. To be empathetic and supportive, don't take on other people's inner life as if it is your own. That's just another way of robbing others of their experience—and of keeping them stuck.

I like to remind my patients: the opposite of depression is *expression*.

What comes out of you doesn't make you sick; what stays in there does.

I recently talked with a beautiful man who counsels children in the Canadian foster care system. He helps young people grieve the loss of family, security, and safety that many never had in the first place. I asked what motivates his work, and he told me about a conversation he had with his father, who was dying of cancer.

"Why do you think you got cancer?" he asked. His father replied, "Because I never learned to cry."

Of course, many factors account for each person's potential for health and disease, and we do great damage to ourselves when we believe we're to blame for our illnesses or injuries. But I can say with certainty that the emotions we don't allow ourselves to express or release stay bottled inside, and whatever we're holding on to affects our body chemistry and finds expression in our cells and neural circuitry. In Hungary we say, "Don't inhale your anger to your breast." It can be harmful to hold on to feelings and keep them locked inside.

Trying to shield others or ourselves from our feelings doesn't work in the long run. But many of us are trained from a young age to disown our inner responses—in other words, to give up our genuine selves. A child says, "I hate school!" and a parent replies, "Hate is a strong word," or "Don't say hate," or "It can't be *that* bad." A child falls down and skins her knee, and a grown-up says, "You're okay!" In trying to help children regroup or bounce back from hurt or difficulty, caring adults can minimize what the child is going through, or inadvertently teach that some things are permissible to feel and others aren't. Sometimes the cues to change or deny a feeling are less subtle: *Calm down! Get over it. Don't be such a crybaby.*

More than by what we say, children learn by watching what we do. If adults create a home environment where anger isn't allowed to be expressed, or where anger is vented in harmful ways, children learn that strong feelings aren't permissible or safe.

Many of us are in the habit of reacting instead of responding to what's going on. We've often learned to hide from our emotions—suppress them, medicate them, run away.

One of my patients, a physician addicted to prescription drugs, called me early one morning. "Dr. Eger," he said, "I realized last night there was no Prozac at Auschwitz." It took me a moment to digest what he'd said. There's a huge difference between self-medicating, as he was doing, and taking necessary medications that have the potential to save lives. But he made a good point. He'd begun reaching outside himself for an escape from his feelings, and he'd become hooked on drugs he didn't need.

At Auschwitz, nothing came from without. There was no way to numb ourselves, to take the edge off, to check out for a while, to forget the reality of torture and hunger and imminent death. We had to learn to be good observers of ourselves and our circumstances. We had to learn to just be.

Yet I don't remember ever crying in the camps. I was too occupied with survival. The feelings came later. And when they came, for many, many years I managed to avoid them, to keep running away.

But you can't heal what you don't feel.

More than thirty years after the war, as part of my ongoing work as a trauma specialist with the US military, I was asked to serve on a prisoner-of-war advisory committee. Every time I visited Washington, DC, to meet with the committee, someone would ask if I'd been to the Holocaust Memorial Museum. I'd already returned to Auschwitz, I'd stood on the ground where I was separated from my parents, under the sky that had received their bodies as they became smoke. Why would I go to a museum

**YOU CAN'T HEAL WHAT YOU DON'T FEEL.**

about Auschwitz and other concentration camps? *Been there, done that*, I thought. For six years I served on the committee, and for six years I avoided setting foot in the museum. And then one morning I was sitting at the mahogany table in our meeting room, my name etched on a little plaque in front of me. And I realized that was then, this is now. I'm Dr. Eger. I made it out.

And as long as I avoided the museum, as long as I convinced myself I'd already overcome the past and had no need to face it again, a part of me was still stuck there. A part of me wasn't free.

So I gathered all my courage and visited the museum. It was every bit as excruciating as I'd feared. I got so flooded with emotion when I saw the photographs of the arrival platform at Auschwitz in May 1944 that I almost couldn't breathe. And then I came to the cattle car. It was a replica of an old German train car built to transport livestock. Visitors could climb inside and feel how dark and small a space it was; feel what it was like to be packed in so tight you were sitting on top of other people; imagine sharing one bucket of water and one bucket for waste with hundreds of people; imagine riding all day and all night without stopping, the only food a stale loaf of bread shared among eight or ten other prisoners. I stood outside the cattle car, completely paralyzed. Frozen. People crowded behind me, waiting quietly, respectfully, for me to step inside. For many minutes I couldn't do it—and then it took every ounce of strength I could muster to coax one foot and then the other through the narrow door.

Inside, a wave of terror came over me and I thought I might vomit. I curled up in a heap, reliving the final days I saw my parents alive. The relentless churn of the wheels on the track.

When I was sixteen, I didn't know we were going to Auschwitz. I didn't know that soon my parents would be dead. I had to survive the discomfort and uncertainty. But somehow, that was easier than reliving it now. This time I had to feel it. This time I cried. I lost track of time sitting there in the dark with my pain, barely noticing as other visitors entered, shared the dark, moved on. I sat for an hour, maybe two.

When I finally got out, I felt different. A little lighter. Emptied out. All my grief and fear weren't gone. Every swastika in every photograph, every hardened eye of an SS officer standing guard made me flinch. But I'd allowed myself to revisit the past and face the feelings I'd been running from for so many years.

There are many good reasons why we avoid our feelings: they're uncomfortable, or they're not the feelings we think we should be having, or we're afraid of how they might hurt others, or afraid of what they could mean—what they might reveal about the choices we've made or the ones we will make going forward.

But as long as you're avoiding your feelings, you're denying reality. And if you try to shut something out and say, "I don't want to think about it," I guarantee that you're going to think about it. So invite the feeling in, sit down with it, keep it company. And then decide how long you're going to hold on to it. Because you're not a fragile little somebody. It's good to

**A FEELING IS JUST A FEELING—IT'S NOT YOUR IDENTITY.**

face every reality. To stop fighting and hiding. To remember that a feeling is just a feeling—it's not your identity.

One September morning sixteen years ago, Caroline was just starting a load of laundry, enjoying a quiet day alone in her house in rural Canada, when there was a knock at the door. She could see through the front window that it was Michael, her husband's cousin. Michael was her age—in his early forties. He had been in trouble much of his life—theft, petty crime, drug abuse—and was finally ready for a second chance. Though he'd recently moved in with his girlfriend, Caroline and her husband had been the family members who'd taken him in to help him turn his life around, setting him up with a job and a stable environment. He'd become a fixture in their lives, another trusted adult who often joined Caroline, her husband, and her three stepsons for dinner.

As much as she cared for Michael and felt good about helping him, for a second Caroline considered pretending she wasn't home. Her husband was out of town, the boys were finally back in school after summer break, and she didn't want Michael's visit to interrupt all the things she'd planned to accomplish on her first morning alone in three months. But it was Michael— a relative she loved, who loved her in return, who relied on her family. She opened the door and invited him in for coffee.

"Boys are back at school already," she said, making small talk as she put the mugs and cream on the table.

"I know."

"Tom's gone, too, for a couple of days."

That's when he pulled out a handgun. He put it to her head, told her to get on the floor. She knelt by the refrigerator.

"What are you doing?" she said. "Michael, what are you doing?"

She could hear him undoing his belt, unzipping his jeans.

Her throat was dry. Her heart pounded. She'd taken a self-defense class in college, and words formed in her mouth, the things she'd been taught to say if someone assaulted you. Use his name. Talk about family. She kept the words coming, her voice somehow sure and steady, talking about Michael's parents, the boys, family holidays, favorite fishing spots.

"Okay, I won't rape you," he finally said. His voice was so off-hand and casual, as though he were saying, "I don't think I'll have any coffee after all."

But he kept the gun pressed to her head. She couldn't see his face. Was he high? What did he want? He seemed to have planned this out, to know he would find her home alone. Was he going to rob her?

"Take anything you want," she said. "You know where to find everything. Just take it, all of it."

"Yeah," he said. "That's what I'm gonna do."

She felt him move, as though ready to step away. Then he stood still again, gun hard against her skull.

"I don't know why I'm doing this," he said.

A noise filled the room. Her head throbbed and burned in pain.

The next thing she knew, she was gaining consciousness. She didn't know how long she'd been passed out on the kitchen floor. She couldn't see anything. She tried to get up, but there was so much blood she kept slipping, falling back down on the floor. She heard footsteps on the basement stairs.

"Michael?" she called out. "Help me!"

It didn't make any sense to ask the person who'd just shot her for help, but it was a reflex. He was family. And there wasn't anyone else there to ask.

"Michael?" she called again.

Another shot rang out. A second bullet blast into the back of her head.

This time, she didn't pass out. This time, she played dead. She lay on the floor, trying not to breathe. She could hear Michael walking around the house. She waited, waited, holding perfectly still. Then the back door closed. Still, she lay on the floor. Maybe he was testing her, tricking her, waiting for her to get up so he could shoot her again. More than pain, more than terror, what she felt was rage. How dare he do this to her? How dare he leave her for dead, leave her for the boys to find when they came home from school? She was damned if she'd let herself die before she could tell someone who'd done this to her, get Michael into custody before he could hurt anyone else.

Finally, the house was completely quiet. She opened her eyes, but she couldn't see anything. The bullets had damaged something in her brain or optic nerve. She crawled unsteadily across the room and pulled herself up to the kitchen counter, feeling around for the phone. She found the receiver, but when she tried to pick it up, it kept slipping from her hands. When she managed to grasp it, she remembered that she couldn't see to dial. She banged randomly at the buttons, dropped the phone, picked it up, tried again. But she couldn't get it to work.

She gave up and crawled slowly, unable to see where she was

going or think what to do. Every once in a while, she'd catch a glimpse of light through the fog of blindness, and eventually she managed to follow the light to the front door, and then outside. They lived on a five-acre lot, the nearest neighbor too far away to hear her if she screamed. She'd have to crawl for help. She made it down the driveway and started up the road of her subdivision, screaming and screaming. She knew someone had finally seen her when she heard a woman let out a bloodcurdling wail, like in a horror film. Soon people came running. Someone shouted to call an ambulance. She could recognize some of her neighbors' voices, but they didn't seem to know who she was. She realized her face was so disfigured and blown apart that they didn't recognize her. She spoke fast, spitting out details: Michael's name, the color of his car, the approximate time when he'd shown up at the house, every detail she could remember. She might not have another chance.

"Call my in-laws," she gasped. "Tell them to make sure the boys are safe at school. Tell Tom and the boys I love them."

Caroline knows her parents and in-laws and stepsons were brought to the hospital to say goodbye, that her father-in-law asked a Catholic priest to come, and her mother brought her Anglican minister. The Catholic priest gave her last rites.

Weeks later, the priest visited her at her in-laws' house, where she was recuperating, and told her, "I've never met anybody who's come back."

"Come back from where?" she asked.

"My darling," he said, "you were cold on the table."

It's truly a miracle that precious Caroline survived.

But if you've lived through a trauma and come out the other side, you know that surviving is only the first battle.

Violence leaves a long and terrible wake. When Caroline reached out to me a few months before Michael was due to be released on parole, almost sixteen years had passed since the shooting, but the psychological wounds were still fresh.

"We see stories on TV," she said, "about a person who suffered a trauma and is coming home. People say, 'We're going to take them home now and make them safe so their lives can go on.' I look at my husband and say, 'If they only knew.' Just because you lived, just because you're going home, life is not magically better. Any person who's been traumatized has a long road to travel."

For Caroline—as for me—some of the residual effects of the trauma are physical. When the swelling on her brain went down, Caroline's vision slowly returned, but she still has upper, lower, and peripheral blindness. She can't hear well. She has nerve deprivation in her hands and arms. When she gets nervous, her brain and body seem disconnected. She has trouble feeling and moving her limbs.

The crime has also taken a toll on her family and community. It's forced everyone to face an evil committed by a loved one, a neighbor, a friend—to suffer a terrible breach of trust. For a long time, Caroline's youngest stepson, who was only eight when this happened, wouldn't leave her alone in a room. She'd try to coax him to join his brothers or the rest of the family, but he'd say, "No, I'll stay here with you. I know you don't like to be alone." When she was able to walk and drive and regain some independence, her oldest stepson became the protective parent, following her around, hovering to make sure she didn't hurt herself. And for a long time, her middle stepson was afraid to hug her or touch her. He was afraid he'd hurt her.

Caroline told me that while some friends and loved ones have coped with the trauma by becoming overprotective, others have dealt with it by minimizing what happened.

"People are often uncomfortable when they know," she said. "They don't want to talk about it. They think if they don't talk about it, that makes it go away. That it's over and done with and we'll just move on. Or they call it my 'accident.' I didn't *accidentally* back into a gun! But people don't want to use words like 'crime' or 'shooting.'"

Even her father-in-law, Michael's uncle—who was present in the aftermath of the shooting, who took Caroline and her family in for three or four months when she couldn't function on her own—would tell people, "She's back to normal, one hundred percent."

"Are you kidding me?" Caroline said with a rueful laugh. "But it made him feel better."

Now, in many ways, stability has returned. The boys are adults, married, a couple with kids of their own. Caroline and her husband live in the US, thousands of miles away from Michael, across an international border, where the chances that he would track them down seeking revenge for her testifying are slim, nearly impossible. But the fear hasn't dissolved.

"He was family," Caroline said. "He lived in our home. We trusted him. And the last thing he said to me was, 'I don't know why I'm doing this.' If he didn't know why he tried to kill me—and he's family—who else out there is going to try to hurt me just because?"

Caroline told me she's scared all the time, always expecting somebody to come and finish what Michael started. She doesn't go outside and garden, something she used to enjoy, because someone could walk up behind her and she wouldn't know they were there. Even indoors she's on constant alert. She doesn't move around her house without an alarm button she can press if someone breaks in. If she misplaces the alarm, she can't breathe until she finds it.

"For a while, I went back and lived in the home where he shot me," she said. "I wasn't going to let him take my home away from me. I was going to take it back."

But it was too terrifying and painful to live in the place where she'd nearly died. They moved far away, to a safe and friendly community in the southern United States, near a beautiful lake where they take their boat on the weekends. Even so, she lives in fear.

"Sixteen years of living like this isn't living," she said.

She felt imprisoned by the past, and she desperately wanted to be free.

As we spoke, I heard so much love and strength and determination in Caroline. I also recognized four behaviors she was practicing that were keeping her stuck in the past and stuck in fear.

For one thing, she was exerting a lot of energy trying to change her feelings, to convince herself to feel differently from the way she actually felt.

"I'm blessed," she said. "I know I'm blessed! I'm alive. I have all these people who love me."

"Yes!" I said. "It's true. But don't try to cheer yourself up when you feel sad. It's not going to help. You're just going to feel guilty, that you should be feeling better than you're feeling. Try this instead. Acknowledge the feeling. It's grief. It's fear. It's sadness. Just acknowledge it. And then give up the need for others' approval. They can't live your life. They can't feel your feelings."

In addition to trying to reason herself out of her very reasonable sadness and fear, Caroline lived in the prison of trying to protect *others* from her feelings. The people who love us want the best for us. They don't want us to hurt. And so it's tempting to show them the version of ourselves they long to see. But when we deny or minimize what we're feeling, it backfires.

Caroline told me that since the shooting, she and her husband had always had dogs, but when their dog died recently, her husband, not understanding how much a dog improved her sense of safety, said he needed time before they brought a new one into their family.

"I was really angry," she said. "But I couldn't tell him that. The logical thing would've been to say, 'I'm afraid to be alone without a dog.' But I wouldn't say it. I think he would understand—but I didn't want him to know I still have that level of fear. I don't know why."

I told her she was protecting him from worry. From guilt. But she was also depriving him, not letting him in. Denying him the opportunity to try to protect her.

Caroline said she was doing the same thing with her sons. "I don't think they know how imprisoned I am. I try not to let them know."

"But you're lying. You're not being the whole you to your family. You're depriving yourself of freedom. And you're depriving them, too. Your strategy for dealing with your difficult emotions has become another problem."

In protecting others from her feelings, Caroline was avoiding taking responsibility for them.

And in remaining consumed by fear, she was giving too much power to Michael and the past.

"My husband and I were just three years married," she said. "We were joining together as a new family, the boys embracing me as their mother, starting a beautiful life. And Michael took it." Her chin stiffened. She clenched her hands into fists.

"He took it?"

"He targeted me. He came to my house with a gun. He put two bullets in my head and left me for dead."

"Yes, he held a gun. Yes, you did what you had to do to stay alive. But nobody can take your inner life or responses from you. Why do you give him more power?"

She'd been victimized in a horrifically cruel and violent way. She had every right to every feeling about it—rage, sorrow, fear, grief. Michael had almost robbed her of her life. But that was sixteen years ago. Even when he was released on parole, he was only a distant threat—far away, with no permission to travel, and no way to find her. Yet she was giving her power away to him, allowing him to live on in her body. She had to get clear of that. To express and release the rage so it didn't continue to pollute her inner life.

I told her to mentally put Michael in a chair, tie him up, beat him. Shout at him. "How could you do this to me?" Get her anger going. Scream it out.

She said she was too afraid to do that.

"The fear was learned. You had no idea what fear was when you were born. Don't let it take over your life. Love and fear don't go together. Enough. You don't have time to live in fear."

"If I get mad at him and beat him—there's going to be nothing left of the chair."

"He was a sick person. Sick people have sick minds. And you get to choose how long you let a sick person's choices keep you from the life you want."

"I don't want to be so scared and sad anymore," she said. "I'm lonely. I've hidden myself away from making new friends and doing new things. I've shut myself in. My face looks tight and worried. I'm always tense and pursed in my mouth. I think my husband would like to have the happy woman back that he married. *I'd* like to have the happy woman back that he married."

> **"NO MORE *DON'T, DON'T, DON'T*. I WANT TO GIVE YOU LOTS OF DOS."**

Sometimes the feelings we run from aren't the uncomfortable or painful ones. Sometimes we avoid the *good* feelings. We shut ourselves off from passion and pleasure and happiness. When we've been victimized, there's a part of our psyche that identifies with the victimizer, and sometimes we adopt that punitive, victimizer stance toward ourselves, denying ourselves the permission to feel good, depriving ourselves of our birthright: joy. That's why I often say that yesterday's victims can easily become today's victimizers.

Whatever you practice, you become better at. If you practice tension, you're going to have more tension. If you practice fear, you'll have more fear. Denial will lead to denying more and more of your truth. Caroline had developed a practice of paranoia. *Don't drive too fast. Don't go too fast in the boat. Don't go there. Don't do that.*

"No more *don't, don't, don't,*" I told her. "I want to give you lots of dos. I *do* have a choice. I *do* have a life to live. I *do* have a role. I *do* live in the present. I *do* pay attention to what I'm focusing on, and it's definitely in alignment with the goals I'm choosing: what gives me pleasure, what gives me joy."

I told Caroline, "I want you to practice engaging and observing your senses—seeing, touching, smelling, tasting. It's time to smile. It's time to laugh. It's time to be lighthearted."

"I'm alive," Caroline said. "I'm so happy I'm alive."

"Yes! Now make sure you practice that happiness every day, every minute, in how you love and talk to yourself."

I gave her one more freedom exercise. I told her to write down what happened, and then go in the backyard with a shovel and start digging a hole. "It's hot," I said, "and you're perspiring. Keep going till you have a hole three feet deep. And bury that piece of paper. Put the soil back over it and go back inside, ready to be born again and have a new beginning because you've put that part to rest."

A month after we spoke, Caroline wrote to tell me she'd been back to Canada to meet her newborn grandson, and she and her husband had driven past their old home, where she had been shot. The oak and maple trees, just slender saplings when they lived there, had grown tall. The new owners had added a front deck. *Somehow, it doesn't hurt my heart as much as it used to*, she wrote. The sadness she harbored for all they left behind had lessened.

This is what it means to face and release the past. We drive on by. We're not living there anymore.

When we're in the habit of denying our feelings, it can be hard even to identify what we're feeling, much less face it, express it, and finally release it. One way we get stuck is by confusing thoughts with feelings. I'm surprised how often I hear people say things like, "I feel I should head downtown this afternoon and run a few errands," or, "I feel like highlights would really brighten your eyes." These aren't feelings! They're thoughts. Ideas. Plans. Feelings are energy. With feelings there's no way out but *through*. We have to be with them. It takes so much courage to be, without having to do anything about anything—to just simply be.

The other day I got a call from a man whose father was struggling with a terminal disease. He asked if I could please visit his father and their family. I've seen many difficult things in my life, but this family's suffering really hit me. The father was confined to a wheelchair and couldn't speak, eat, or move his own body, and his wife and son were so scared, jumping up and down to reposition his arms or legs or blankets, doing what they could to mitigate his discomfort—but powerless to halt the progress of his illness.

I didn't know what would be useful for him or the family. I was quiet. I asked his wife to hold his hand, to give him a kiss, and just be. I held the father's other hand. Our eyes met, and I could see all his feelings of powerlessness and helplessness. By simply being present, we gave him permission for it all to come to the surface, without judgment. Together, we did our best to become comfortable with discomfort. We sat together for a long time.

The son called four days later to say that his father had passed. I shared that I felt I had done little to support them, and yet, the son was insistent I had helped them immensely. Perhaps what they found useful was the opportunity to practice presence. To sit with each other and with the disease and with our mortality, without succumbing to the need to fix or change any part of it.

Inspired by this family, I managed to do something I've never been able to do before. I hate to be confined or tied down, because it sends me careening into panic. For procedures like MRIs, I've always asked to be sedated. But last week I decided to try my next routine MRI—I must have them to check my back—without any medication to relax me.

An MRI machine is dark and confining—and extremely loud. I was put inside and the noise started up. Lying there in my thin hospital gown in the tube, my crooked spine pressed against the cold plastic pad, I felt fear slice through me. The banging was so loud it sounded like bombers were coming to deliver a blast, like the whole building might collapse in a heap of rubble. I thought I was going to scream and kick and have to be pulled out. But I said to myself, "The more noise I hear, the more relaxed I become." And I did it. I made it for forty minutes in that machine without a pill. The ability to be still with my discomfort didn't happen overnight. But as the years pass, I keep practicing.

This is how we release ourselves from the prison of avoidance— we let the feelings come. We let them move through us. And then we let them go.

# KEYS TO FREE YOURSELF FROM AVOIDANCE

- **Feel so you can heal.** Develop a daily practice of checking in on your feelings. Pick a neutral time—for example, when you're sitting down to a meal, waiting in the checkout line at the grocery store, or brushing your teeth. Take a few deep breaths and ask yourself, "What am I feeling right now?" Scan your body for sensations like tightness, tingling, pleasure, or pain. See if you can identify a feeling and just name it, without judgment or trying to change it.

- **Everything is temporary.** When observing your feelings at neutral times becomes a comfortable habit, next try tuning into your feelings when you are flooded by a strong emotion, positive or negative. If you can, step away from the situation or interaction that is provoking the feeling of joy, sorrow, anger, and so on. Sit in stillness for a moment and breathe—it might help to close your eyes or lightly rest your hands on your lap or abdomen. Start by naming your feeling. Then, see if you can locate the feeling in your body. Get curious about it. Is it hot or cold? Loose or tight? Does it burn or ache or throb? Finally, observe how the feeling changes or dissipates.

- **The opposite of depression is expression.** Think of a recent conversation with a friend, partner, colleague, or family member when you avoided saying what you were feeling. It isn't too late to take responsibility for your feelings and express your truth. Tell the person *that you've been reflecting on the conversation and would like to follow up. Arrange a convenient time to speak, and say something like, "You know, I didn't know how to express this at the time, but I realize I was feeling ___ when ___."*

# CHAPTER 3

# All Other Relationships Will End

## The Prison of Self-Neglect

One of our first fears is of abandonment. Thus we learn early how to get the A's: attention, affection, approval. We figure out what to do and whom to become to get our needs met. The problem is not that we do these things—it's that we keep doing them. We think we must in order to be loved.

It's very dangerous to put your whole life into someone else's hands. *You* are the only one you're going to have for a lifetime. All other relationships will end. So how can you be the best loving, unconditional, no-nonsense caregiver to yourself?

In childhood, we receive all sorts of messages—spoken and unspoken—that shape our beliefs about how we matter and what we're worth. And we can carry these messages into adulthood.

For example, Brian's father abandoned the family when Brian was ten, and he became the man of the house, taking care of his mother, doing everything in his power to make life easier for her, to soothe her pain—and to make sure she wouldn't leave, too. He brought this caretaker identity into adulthood and kept choosing relationships with needy women. He resented them for the constant sacrifice they demanded, and yet he had difficulty setting healthy boundaries. He thought that to be loved, he had to be needed.

Another patient, Matthew, was born to a mother who had not chosen to become pregnant with him. She felt burdened by motherhood and entered into it with no sense of anticipation or enthusiasm. When parents are stressed or disappointed or unfulfilled, their children pick up the tab, carrying the burden into their own lives. As an adult, Matthew still held a terrible fear of abandonment that manifested in rage. He was cruel to his girlfriends, and would go on rants in public, yelling at people, once even throwing a dog across a parking lot. He was so afraid of being left that he turned the fear into a self-fulfilling prophecy, behaving in such a way that people had no choice but to step away from him. Then he could say, "I knew it all along." He became who he dreaded in an attempt to control his fear of abandonment.

Even if we didn't experience a discernible event or trauma that forced us to fight to be loved or seen, most of us can remember times we protected others or performed for them in order to secure their approval. We may have come to believe that we're loved for our achievements, or for the role we fill in the family, or because we take care of others.

Unfortunately, many families, in trying to motivate children to do well for themselves, create a culture of achievement in which the child's "being" gets entwined with her "doing"; she's taught she matters not for who she is, but for how she performs and behaves. Children are under such intense pressure to get good grades, be high-performing athletes or musicians, ace college entrance tests, earn a degree at a select college or university that will lead to a high-paying job in a competitive field. But if a good report card or good manners earn love, that's not love at all. It's manipulation. When so much emphasis is placed on achievement, children don't get to experience unconditional love—that they're loved no matter what, that they're free to be themselves, that it's permissible to make mistakes, that we're all in a process of learning and becoming, and that learning can be exciting and joyful.

My grandson Jordan is a photographer, and he was recently hired to take portraits at an acting studio in Los Angeles. A director who just days earlier had won two Oscars was visiting the acting class that day. Someone asked him where he had decided to display his trophies, and he surprised everyone by admitting he'd tucked them away in a drawer. "I don't want my kids to come home from school every day," he said, "and see my Oscars and think, *What am I possibly going to do to compare?*" I laughed when Jordan told me this, because he is also the son of an extraordinarily successful man. His father, Marianne's husband, Rob, won a Nobel Prize in economics. And Rob also keeps his prize in a drawer, tossed in next to the wine opener!

There's no need to hide our success from our children. But this director and my precious Rob have a lovely way of acknowledging that their awards and accomplishments are not *who* they are. They don't confuse who they are with what they do. When we conflate achievement with worth, success as well as disappointment can become a burden on our children.

Marianne told me a sweet story that's a good reminder of a very different legacy we can choose to pass on. My oldest great-grandson—her grandson Silas—came to stay with Marianne and Rob in New York one weekend. He said, "Granny, I heard that Papa won a big, important award." He asked to see it. Marianne pulled it out of the drawer and Silas stared at it for a long time, running his finger over his grandfather's name etched into the gold plaque: Robert Fry Engle, III. Finally, he said, "My middle name is Frye. Why does it say Fry?" Marianne said, "Well, who do you think you're named after?" Silas was delighted to discover that part of his name came from his grandfather. Later, a family friend came over for dinner and Silas proudly asked, "Have you seen my prize?" He ran to the drawer and pulled it out. "See?" he said. "My name's on it. Papa and I have a prize!"

It's not good to live with success looming over you, feeling burdened by the need to reach a certain height to be worthy of love. And yet the strengths and skills of our ancestors are also a part of us. It's our legacy. It's our prize, too. We honor our children when we can create a culture not of self-aggrandizement or self-effacement, of overachievement or underachievement—but a culture of the *joy* of achievement. The joy of working hard. Of nurturing our gifts. Not because we have to. Because we're free to. Because we're blessed with the gift of life.

My daughter Audrey and her son David have taught me so much about nurturing gifts rather than fulfilling expectations.

David is an incredibly bright and creative person. As soon as he could read, he had a photographic memory for sports stats. I'll never forget watching *The Wizard of Oz* with him when he was two and he deduced that the woman riding her bicycle in the storm was the Wicked Witch. But while he excelled in extra-curricular activities in high school—playing soccer, writing songs, performing with the choir, starting the school's first comedy club—and scored very high on standardized tests, his grades were a problem. Audrey and her husband, Dale, were often called into the counselor's office because David was in danger of failing classes. His senior year, when he was accepted at two small private colleges, he reluctantly told his parents that he didn't feel ready to go.

Education has always been a strong value in our family—in part because Béla and I missed opportunities when our lives were interrupted by war. But Audrey didn't guilt David or lay down the law. She listened. And when she learned about a new music academy opening in Austin, where they live, she told David that if he could get in, he could take a gap year to focus on music, and then figure out his college plans. He jumped on the opportunity, recorded a demo of original songs, and earned a spot at the music school.

Taking time to focus on something he loved and was good at—and feeling supported by his parents in doing things at his own speed, in his own way—gave David the focus and motivation to later pursue a career path he cared about. When he did go to college—on a choir scholarship—he knew what he wanted to do, and he genuinely wanted to be there. He was making a choice that served him, not just doing what he had to do to fulfill someone else's expectation. Now he has a journalism degree and a job he loves as a sportswriter. And music continues to be an important and joyful part of his life. I'm moved and impressed by Audrey and Dale's parenting, and by David's capacity to know and express his truth.

Too often we're boxed in by expectations, by the sense that we have a specific role or function to fulfill. Often in families, children are given a label: the responsible child, the jokester, the rebel. When we give children a name, they play the game. And when there's a "best" in the family—a high achiever or good girl or good boy—there's usually a "best worst." As one of my patients put it, "My brother was very disruptive as a child. The way I got attention was being cooperative and being good." But a label is not an identity.

> **TOO OFTEN WE'RE BOXED IN BY EXPECTATIONS, BY THE SENSE THAT WE HAVE A SPECIFIC ROLE OR FUNCTION TO FULFILL.**

It's a mask—or a prison. My patient said it beautifully: "You can only be the good girl for so long. Bubbling under the surface, my real personality was trying to get out and my environment wasn't encouraging of that." Our childhoods end when we begin to live in someone else's image of who we are.

Instead of limiting ourselves to one role or version of ourselves, it's good to recognize that each of us has an entire family inside. There's the childish part, the one who wants everything now and fast and easy. There's the childlike part—the curious free spirit, adept at following whims, instincts, and desires without judgment or fear or shame. There's the teenager who likes to flirt and risk and test boundaries. There's the rational adult who thinks things through, makes plans, sets goals, figures out how to reach them. And there are the two parents: the caring parent and the scaring parent. The one who is kind and loving and nurturing, and the one who comes in with voice raised and finger wagging, who says, "You should, you must, you have to." We need our entire inner family to be whole. And when we're free, this family works in balance, as a team, everyone welcome, no one absent or silenced or ruling the roost.

My inner free spirit helped me survive Auschwitz, but without my responsible adult on board, she can make a lot of messes, as my granddaughter Rachel—Audrey's beautiful daughter—can attest. Since she was young, Rachel has loved to cook, and it warmed my heart when she asked if I'd teach her some Hungarian recipes. I decided to show her how to make one of my favorite dishes: chicken paprikash. It was a special kind of heaven to be in the kitchen with Rachel, the smell of onions sautéing in butter (*a lot* of butter!) and chicken fat. But soon I noticed her father, Dale, at my elbow, wiping up the spatters of schmaltz and dustings of spice that flew from my spoon. Even patient, down-to-earth Rachel was growing exasperated. "Stop!" she finally said, grabbing my arm before I threw a bunch of garlic and paprika into the pot. "If I'm going to learn the recipe, I have to measure and write down how much you're putting in."

I didn't want to slow down. I love to cook by instinct, to let go of measuring and planning and just go by heart. But that wasn't giving Rachel the foundation she needed. To effectively pass down my strength and skills, I couldn't rely on my inner free spirit alone. I needed my inner rational adult and caring parent in the room to round out the team.

Now, Rachel makes the best chicken paprikash and szekely goulash, and when I made a nut roll the other day, I had to call her to tell me whether to add a half or full cup of water to the dough. She didn't have to look at the recipe. "It's a half cup!" she said.

\*　　\*　　\*

It can be especially challenging to balance our inner family when we think our very survival depends on filling a specific role. After decades of maintaining an unhealthy pattern with her sisters and parents, Iris is trying to break out of the confining role she grew accustomed to filling in her family.

Her father served in WWII and was discharged from the army after a tank he'd worked on exploded with men on board. He became a psychiatric nurse, but began drinking heavily and suffering from depression, paranoia, and schizophrenia, so much so that by the time Iris, the youngest of four children, was born, he regularly spent large stretches of time in the hospital. She remembers him as a gentle, sensitive, brilliant man. She loved to sit in his lap after her bath and have him comb the tangles out of her wet hair. Or she would pretend to fall asleep on the couch in the evenings so he'd carry her up to bed. It felt good to be in his arms. When she was twelve, he had a massive heart attack. By the time the ambulance arrived, his heart had been stopped for twelve minutes. The medical team managed to revive him, but he was severely brain damaged and became a permanent resident at the same hospital where he'd once worked. He died when she was eighteen.

At a young age, Iris learned to fill the caregiver role in her family. In one of her earliest memories, her parents had been in a heavy discussion. She could sense the tension and slipped into the room, hoping to lighten the mood. Her father scooped her up and held her. "You're my favorite," he said. "You don't cause any trouble."

This message was reinforced by Iris's mother and sisters. She earned the A's in her family by being the responsible one, the person others could depend on. Her mother, a hardworking, nonjudgmental person always sensitive to the hurt or shame or embarrassment underlying others' behavior, remained steadfastly loyal to Iris's father throughout his worst years, but had a nervous breakdown when Iris was a teenager. Years later, when she herself was ailing, she told Iris, "I feel I'm in the middle of a stormy sea, and you're my rock."

Much of Iris and her mother's relationship centered around their mutual concern for Iris's sisters, who'd endured rough and chaotic lives, suffering among them the traumas of sexual abuse and domestic violence, as well as struggles with addiction and suicidal depression. Iris and her sisters are now in their fifties, and she continues to grapple with complex feelings that stem in large part from her caretaking role in the family.

"I live with a huge feeling of responsibility in my heart," she told me. "I was called 'the lucky one.' I didn't experience abuse. My father was away in the mental hospital when I was very little and he was at his most crazy. I've never wanted to take my own life. I'm happily married to a kind man and have three wonderful children, now adults. I feel guilty at times about the good things that have come my way. I feel heartbreak for my sisters. I feel selfish for not doing more for them. And I'm exhausted at times—maybe from trying to maintain security, or live life as the girl who didn't cause any trouble because everyone else's problems were so much bigger. I daydream about winning the lotto and buying them each a house, setting them up financially for the rest of their lives. Then I might feel freer of this guilt I carry."

Iris is a beautiful woman, with blond curly hair and full lips. She seemed preoccupied, her blue eyes darting as she spoke—the agitation that comes from a life of trying to earn the A's.

Iris had imprisoned herself in her perception of her role and identity: to make things better for others, to lighten the load, to not cause a fuss or have big problems, to be the capable, dependable, responsible one. She had also become a prisoner of guilt—survivor's guilt for her journey being easier than her mother's and sisters'. How could I guide Iris out of a life of patterning herself as the responsible "good girl" and wishing she could fix others?

"You can't do anything for your sisters," I told her, "until you start loving yourself."

"I don't know how," she said. "This year I've had hardly any contact with them. And I'm relieved, which feels terrible. I worry about them. Are they okay? Could I do more? And I *could* do more. That's the truth. And yet, when I do more, it becomes toxic and all-consuming. So I'm in a mess. I don't know how to move on.

"I'm lost about how to re-form any connection," she said. "And I'm torn, because while I do want to reconnect with them, when I'm really honest with myself, it's so much easier when we're not in touch. And that feels awful."

There were two things I hoped she could let go of: guilt and worry. "Guilt is in the past," I told her. "Worry is in the future. The only thing you can change is right here in the present. And it's not up to you to decide what to do for your sisters. The only one you can love and accept is *you*. The question isn't how can you love your sisters enough. It's how you can love *yourself* enough."

**"GUILT IS IN THE PAST. WORRY IS IN THE FUTURE."**

She nodded, but I saw hesitation in her eyes, something held back in her smile, as though the very thought of loving herself was uncomfortable—or at least unfamiliar.

68

"Honey, when you concentrate on what more you can do for your sisters, it isn't healthy. It's not healthy for you. And it's not healthy for *them*. You cripple them. You make them depend on you. You deprive them of being responsible grown-ups."

I suggested that maybe they weren't the ones with the need. Maybe *she* was. Sometimes we have the need to be needed. We don't feel we're functioning well if we're not rescuing people. But when you depend on being needed, you're likely to marry an alcoholic. They're irresponsible, you're responsible. You re-create that pattern.

I told Iris, "This is a good time for you to marry *you*. Otherwise, you're going to make a bad situation worse, not better."

She was quiet, her expression disoriented. "That's so hard," she said. "I still feel guilty."

When they were children, her eldest sister was very angry and frightening. At the time, no one knew she had experienced sexual abuse. Iris would come home from school and lock herself in her bedroom to avoid her sister's volatility. She and the other sisters would beg their parents, "Can't you get rid of her? Can't you control her?" One day the eldest sister had an enormous fight with their father and pushed him through a screen door. That was when their parents sent her to a girls' home—and from there, her life became ever rockier.

"I might have been the reason my parents chose to send her away," Iris said.

"If you want to have a loving relationship with your sisters," I said, "it can't be based on needing each other. It's because you *want* each other. So, you can choose. Do you want to have guilt, or do you want to have love?"

To choose love is to become kind and good and loving *for you*.

To stop rehashing the past. To stop apologizing for not being there to save everyone. It means saying, "I did the best I could."

"But it feels like part of my whole life journey is to somehow find a solution to what happened to the three of us," Iris said. "As the only person in my family who didn't have a major struggle, I was the only one who could keep it together back then. And now I feel disloyal when I'm not helping them."

One of the first questions I ask patients is, "When did your childhood end?" When did you start protecting or taking care of someone else? When did you stop being yourself, and start filling a role?

I told Iris, "You may have grown up very fast. You became a little adult, taking care of other people, being the responsible one. And feeling guilty that no matter what you did, nothing was enough."

She nodded, tears filling her eyes.

"So now you decide: when is enough enough?"


It's difficult to relinquish our old ways of earning the A's and discover a new way to build love and connection, one that hinges on interdependence, not dependence; on love, not need.

When I'm trying to help a patient get at his or her early patterning I often ask, "Is there anything you do in excess?" We often use substances and behaviors to medicate our wounds: food, sugar, alcohol, shopping, gambling, sex. We can even do healthy things in excess. We can become addicted to work or exercise or restrictive diets. But when we're hungry for affection, attention, and approval—for the things we didn't get when we were young—nothing is ever going to be enough to fill the need.

You're going to the wrong place to fill the void. It's like going to the hardware store to buy a banana. The thing you're looking for isn't there. And yet, many of us keep going to the wrong store.

Sometimes we get addicted to needing. Sometimes we get addicted to being needed.

Lucia is a nurse, and she told me she thinks it's in her genetic code to focus on others, to ask, "What do you need? How can I help?" It took decades of marriage to a demanding man, stepping in to raise his children, including a

**IT'S GOOD TO BE *SELF*-ISH: TO PRACTICE SELF-LOVE AND SELF-CARE.**

daughter with disabilities, years of being told "Do this! Do that!" before she started to ask, "What about me? Who am I in this situation?"

Now she's learning to be more assertive, to stop disconnecting from her own preferences and desires. Sometimes it garners a rocky response from others. The first time she set a boundary with her husband, refusing to get up from the couch to fix him a snack, he yelled, "I ordered you!"

She took a deep, stabilizing breath, and said, "I don't take orders. If you speak to me that way again, I'll leave the room."

She's learning to recognize that the clinching feeling at the top of her gut when she starts to say yes to a request is a signal to stop and ask herself, "Is this what I want to do? Will I be resentful if I do this?"

It's good to be *self*-ish: to practice self-love and self-care.

When Lindsey and Jordan were young, Marianne and Rob made a commitment to give each other solo nights away from the family scene. On Marianne's night out, Rob agreed to be home with the kids, and vice versa. One week a famous economist was going to be visiting from London, and Rob wanted to hear him speak. But the event was on Marianne's night out; she'd already purchased tickets to see a play with a friend, and he'd already made a commitment to be home with the kids. When he told Marianne he couldn't find a babysitter on such short notice, she could have called her friend to reschedule, and contacted the theater to try to exchange their tickets for another night. We can always make the choice to accommodate, to be flexible. The problem is that many of us rush to fix and adjust out of habit. We take too much responsibility for others' problems, training them to rely on us instead of on themselves, and paving our own way toward resentment down the road. Marianne gave Rob a kiss on the cheek and said, "Gosh, hon, it sounds like you have a dilemma. I hope you can figure it out." In the end, he brought the children with him to the lecture and they played under the auditorium chairs in their pajamas.

**LOVE IS A FOUR-LETTER WORD SPELLED T-I-M-E.**

Sometimes life requires us to go with the flow, sometimes it's the right thing to prioritize others' needs, to modify our plans. And of course, we want to do everything in our power to support our loved ones, to be sensitive to their needs and desires, to engage in teamwork and interdependence. But generosity isn't generous if we chronically give at the expense of ourselves, if our giving makes us a martyr or fuels our resentment. Love means that we practice self-love, that we strive to be generous and compassionate toward others—*and* to ourselves.

I often say that love is a four-letter word spelled T-I-M-E.

Time. While our inner resources are limitless, our time and energy are limited. They run out. If you work or are in school; if you have children, a relationship, friends; if you volunteer, exercise, or belong to a book club, support group, or house of worship; if you're caring for an aging parent or someone with medical or special needs—how do you structure your time so you don't neglect yourself? When do you rest and replenish? How do you create a balance between working, loving, and playing?

Sometimes the hardest way to show up for ourselves is to ask for help. For a few years I've been dating a gentle man and a gentleman, Gene, my wonderful swing dance partner. When he had to be in the hospital for a few weeks, I visited every day, and he was happy to let me baby him a little—hold his hand, spoon-feed him meals. It's wonderful when someone gives you the gift of giving. I was sitting with him one afternoon and noticed he was shivering. He admitted he'd been quite cold, but for Gene, kindness is number one, and he was so worried about coming across as demanding that he'd decided not to ask for a warmer blanket. In trying not to be a burden on anyone else, he neglected himself.

I used to do that, too. In our early immigrant days, Béla and I lived with Marianne in a tiny maid's apartment at the back of a house in Park Heights, Baltimore. We had arrived in the country penniless—we had to borrow the ten dollars to get off the boat—and struggled to feed our family. In tough circumstances, I held it as a point of pride to put food on Béla and Marianne's plates first—to serve myself only if there was enough to go around. It's true that generosity and compassion are vital to foster. But selflessness doesn't serve anyone—it leaves everyone deprived.

And being self-reliant doesn't mean you refuse care and love from others.

Audrey was home for a visit during her college years at the University of Texas, Austin, a hotbed of activism and progressive politics. She opened my bedroom door on a Saturday morning and was horrified to find me in bed in my designer nightgown, Béla feeding me bites of fresh papaya.

"Mother!" she cried. I was disgusting to her in that moment—froufrou, dependent. I'd offended her sensibilities of what it means to be a woman of strength.

What she didn't see was the choice I'd made, to honor and embrace my husband's delight in caring for me. He lived for Saturdays when he'd get up early and drive across the border to the produce market in Juarez and search for the ripest red papayas that I loved. It brought him joy. And it brought me joy, too, to share in the sensory ritual, to receive what he longed to give.

When you're free, you take responsibility for being who you really are. You recognize the coping mechanisms or behavior patterns you've adopted in the past to get your needs met. You reconnect with the parts of yourself you had to give up, and reclaim the whole person you weren't allowed to be. You break the habit of abandoning yourself.

Remember: you have something no one else will ever have. You have you. For a lifetime.

That's why I talk to myself all the time. I say, "Edie, you're one of a kind. You're beautiful. May you be more and more Edie every day."

I am no longer in the habit of denying myself, emotionally or physically. I'm proud to be a high-maintenance woman! My wellness regimen includes acupuncture and massage. I do regular beauty treatments that aren't necessary but feel good. I

**BREAK THE HABIT OF ABANDONING YOURSELF.**

have facials. I get my hair painted—not just dyed one color, but three, from dark to light. I go to the department store makeup counter and experiment with new ways of doing my eyes. If I hadn't learned to develop inner self-regard, no amount of pampering on the outside could change the way I feel about myself. But now that I hold myself in high esteem, now that I love myself, I know that taking care of myself on the inside can include taking care of myself on the outside, too—treating myself to nice things without suffering guilt, letting my appearance be an avenue for self-expression. And I've learned to accept a compliment. When someone says, "I like your scarf," I say, "Thank you. I like it, too."

I'll never forget the day I took teenage Marianne clothes shopping and she tried on an outfit I'd picked out for her and said, "Mom, it's not me." Her comment startled me. I worried I had raised her to be picky or even ungrateful. But then I realized what a gift it is to have children who know their own minds, who know what is "me" and what is "not me."

Honey, find *you* and keep filling it up with more you. You don't have to work to be loved. You just have to be *you*. May you be more and more you every day.

# KEYS TO FREE YOURSELF
# FROM SELF-NEGLECT

- *Anything we practice, we become better at.* Spend at least five minutes every day savoring pleasant sensations: the first sip of coffee in the morning, the feel of warm sun on your skin or a hug from someone you love, the sound of laughter or rain on the roof, the smell of baking bread. Take time to notice and experience joy.

- *Work, love, play.* Make a chart that shows your waking hours each day of the week. Label the time you spend every day working, loving, and playing. (Some activities might fit in more than one category; if so, use all the labels that apply.) Then add up the total hours you spend working, loving, and playing in a typical week. Are the three categories roughly in balance? How could you structure your days differently so you do more of whatever is currently receiving the least of your time?

- *Show yourself some love.* Reflect on a time within the last week when someone demanded something of you or asked you for a favor. How did you respond? Was your response out of habit? Necessity? Desire? How did your response feel in your body? Was your response good for you? Now reflect on a time within the last week when you asked—or wanted to ask—someone for help. What did you say? How did it work out? Was your response good for you? What can you do today to be self-ish—to show yourself love and care?

# CHAPTER 4

# One Butt,
# Two Chairs

# The Prison of Secrets

In Hungary we have an expression: *If you sit with one butt on two chairs, you become half-assed.*

If you're living a double life, it's going to catch up with you.

When you're free, you're able to live with authenticity, to stop straddling the gap between two chairs—your ideal self and your real self—and become congruent. You learn to sit fully in the chair of your own fulfillment.

Robin was struggling in the gap between two chairs when she came to see me, her marriage on the brink of collapse. She'd grown exhausted trying to live up to her husband's exacting demands, and their marriage had become passionless and empty. She felt she needed an oxygen mask just to get through the day. In search of relief and joy, she began an affair.

Cheating is a dangerous game. Nothing is more exciting than

a new lover. When you're in a new bed, you're not talking about who's going to take out the garbage, whose turn it is to drive the carpool to soccer practice. It's all pleasure, no responsibility. And it's temporary. For a while after the affair began, Robin had felt alive to joy, more optimistic, more nourished, able to tolerate the status quo at home because her hunger for affection and intimacy was being fed elsewhere. But then her lover gave her an ultimatum. She had to choose: her husband, or him.

She booked her first session with me because she was stuck, unable to make up her mind. At her first appointment, she went around and around, detailing the pros and cons of two seemingly impossible choices. While a divorce would keep her lover from leaving, it would devastate her two children. But if she stayed in the marriage, she'd have to give up the one person who made her feel seen and cherished. It was either her kids' happiness or her own fulfillment.

But the fundamental choice she needed to make wasn't about which man to be with. Whatever she was doing with her husband—withdrawing, hiding, keeping secrets—she would continue to do with the lover, or in any romantic relationship, until she chose to change. Her freedom wasn't about choosing the right man. It was about finding a way to express her desires, hopes, and fears in any relationship.

Sadly, this is a common problem. Even a marriage begun with passion and connection can grow to feel like a prison cell. It happens slowly over time, and it's often difficult to see when and how the bars are built. There are the usual intrusions—stress over money or work or children or extended family or illness— and because the couple lacks the time or the tools to resolve these irritations, the worry and hurt and anger build up. After a while it's even harder to express these feelings, because they lead to tension or arguments, and so it's preferable to avoid the topics altogether. Before two people know it, they're living separate lives. The door is open for someone else to come in and attempt to fill what's been lost.

When a relationship is strained, it's not one person's fault. Both people are doing things to maintain the distance and disputes. Robin's husband was a perfectionist. He criticized her and was judgmental and hard to please. At first, it was tough for her to recognize that she was also doing things to damage the relationship: pulling away, going to another room, disengaging, disappearing. Most of all, keeping her unhappiness a secret. The affair was a secondary secret. The primary secret was all that she had begun habitually concealing from her husband—her daily ups and downs, sorrows and pleasures, longing and grief.

**HONESTY STARTS WITH LEARNING TO TELL THE TRUTH TO YOURSELF.**

Honesty starts with learning to tell the truth to yourself.

I told Robin I would keep treating her if she liked, but only if she put the affair on hold as she worked to be in a more honest relationship with herself.

I gave her two exercises. The first I call Vital Signs. It's a quick way of taking your own temperature, becoming aware of your inner climate and the emotional weather you're putting into the world. We're always communicating, even when we're not saying a word. The only time we don't communicate is when we're in a coma. Several times a day, make a conscious effort to check in with your body, to ask yourself, "Do I feel soft and warm, or cold and stiff?"

Robin didn't like discovering how often she was stiff, rigid, closed off. Over time, the act of taking her emotional temperature helped her soften. This is when I introduced the second exercise, Pattern Interruption—a way to consciously replace a habitual response with something else. When Robin felt herself wanting to withdraw or withhold from her husband, she would make a conscious effort not to disappear. She'd soften her gaze and look at her husband with loving eyes—something she hadn't done for a long time. One evening at the dinner table, she gently reached for his hand.

It was a tiny step toward intimacy. They still had a lot of repairs to make if they were to rebuild their relationship. But they'd begun.

Healing can't happen as long as we're hiding or disowning parts of ourselves. The things we silence or cover up become like hostages in the basement, trying more and more desperately to get our attention.

I know because I tried to hide my past for years, to conceal what had happened to me, to hide my grief and rage. When Béla and I fled Communist Europe after the war and came to America with Marianne, I wanted to be normal. I didn't want to be the shipwrecked person I was, a mother who was also a Holocaust survivor. I worked in a garment factory, cutting loose threads off the seams of little boys' underwear, paid seven cents per dozen, too scared to say anything in English for fear others would hear my accent. I just wanted to fit in, to be accepted. I didn't want people to feel sorry for me. I didn't want my scars to show.

It wasn't until decades later, when I was finishing my training as a clinical psychologist, that I realized the cost of my double life. I was trying to heal others without healing myself. I was an impostor. On the outside, I was a doctor. On the inside, a terrified sixteen-year-old was quaking, cloaked in denial, over-achievement, and perfectionism.

Until I could face the truth, I had my secret, and my secret had me.

My secret also had my children, in ways I'm still growing to understand. The childhood memories Marianne, Audrey, and John have shared—the fear and tension they sensed under the surface without knowing what it was about—are similar to what I've read in letters from readers around the world who are children of Holocaust survivors.

Ruth, whose parents were Hungarian survivors, told me about the impact her parents' silence had on her growing up. On the one hand, she had a wonderful childhood. Her father and mother were outwardly joyful and relieved to have immigrated to Australia, happy to be able to offer their children a good education, to send them to ballet and piano classes, to raise them in a peaceful environment, to celebrate their accomplishments and friendships. "We're lucky," they'd often say. "Thank goodness." There was no obvious stamp of trauma.

But there was a disconnect between Ruth's inner and outer

experience. Her parents' positivity about the present in contrast with their silence about the past left her feeling anxious. A sense of foreboding threaded its way through many experiences, however pleasurable or mundane. Picking up on her parents' unspoken trauma and fear, she, too, developed a belief that something was wrong, that something terrible was about to happen. She became a successful psychiatrist and a mother, but no matter how accomplished she was, she harbored a chronic sense of dread and asked, *Why do I feel this way?* Even her professional training in psychiatry didn't give her the right lens to understand.

When he turned nineteen, Ruth's youngest son asked her to take him and his brother to Hungary. He wanted to learn more about his grandparents, who were no longer alive. And with the rise of right-wing extremism around the globe, and an understanding that those who don't know history are doomed to repeat it, he felt especially committed to knowing more about the past. But Ruth balked. She'd been to Hungary as a young woman, during the height of Communism, and it had not been a pleasant experience. She had no desire to return.

Then a friend recommended a book to her—*The Choice!*—and reading it gave her new courage and a strong imperative to face her parents' past. She agreed to the trip.

It turned out that retracing her parents' past with her sons was an intensely transformative and healing experience. They visited a synagogue that houses an exhibition on the Budapest ghetto. For the first time, she saw pictures that detailed what her mother had lived through. It was painful and difficult to take in the truth. But it was also helpful and empowering. She

gained insight and a new sense of connection to her parents—
she understood why they'd been so reluctant to talk about the
past, appreciating that they were trying to protect her, and
themselves. But hiding or minimizing our truth doesn't protect
our loved ones. Protecting them means working to heal the past
so we don't inadvertently pass the trauma on to them. As Ruth
confronted her family's legacy, she was able to feel congruence
within herself. To come to terms with the root of her anxiety
and begin to release it.

My healing didn't start until a fellow student at the University of Texas gave me a copy of Viktor Frankl's *Man's Search
for Meaning* and I finally worked up the courage to read it. I
had so many excuses, so many reasons to resist: *I don't need to
read someone else's account of Auschwitz,* I told myself. *I was
there! Why feel the pain all over again? Why open myself up to
nightmares? Why revisit hell?* But when I finally cracked the
book open in the middle of the night while my family slept
and the house was quiet, something unexpected happened: I
felt seen. Frankl had been where I'd been. It felt like he was
speaking directly to me. Our experiences weren't identical.
He was in his thirties when he was imprisoned, already an
acclaimed psychiatrist; I was a sixteen-year-old gymnast and
ballet student dreaming of my boyfriend. But the way he wrote
about our shared past changed my life. I saw a new possibility
for myself—a way to give up secrets and hiding, to stop fighting and running away from the past. His words—and later,
his mentorship—gave me the courage and inspiration to face

and express my truth, and in speaking my secret, reclaim my genuine self.

Reckoning and release are impossible when we keep secrets—when we operate under a code of denial, delusion, or minimization.

Sometimes the demand to keep a secret is unspoken or unconscious. Sometimes others buy our silence with threats or force. Either way, secrets are harmful because they create and sustain a climate for shame, and shame is the bottom line of any addiction. Freedom comes from facing and telling the truth—and, as I'll explore in the next chapter, this is only possible when we create a climate of love and acceptance within ourselves.

# KEYS TO FREE YOURSELF
# FROM SECRETS

- *If you sit with one butt on two chairs, you become half-assed.* Place two chairs side by side. Begin by sitting on one chair, legs uncrossed. Feel the way your feet rest against the floor. Feel your sit bones heavy on the chair. Feel your spine lengthen out of your pelvis, your head extend from your neck. Soften your shoulders away from your ears. Take a few deep, nourishing breaths, lengthening with the inhale, grounding with the exhale. Now move so you are sitting with one butt cheek on one chair, the other cheek on the other chair. Check in with your feet, your sit bones, your spine, neck, head, and shoulders. How do your body and breath feel when you straddle two chairs? Finally, return to one chair. Ground your feet and sit bones. Lengthen your spine and neck. You're back home. Follow your breath as you realign and become congruent.

- *Honesty starts with learning to tell the truth to yourself.* Try the Vital Signs exercise that Robin used to heal her marriage. Several times a day, make a conscious effort to check in with your body and take your own emotional temperature. Ask yourself, "Do I feel soft and warm, or cold and stiff?"

- *Tell the truth in the safe presence of others.* Support groups and twelve-step programs can be a wonderful place to share your truth—and learn from others who *are doing the same. Find a local or online meeting where you will be in the company of people who can relate to and empathize with your experience. Attend at least three meetings before you decide whether or not it's for you.*

# CHAPTER 5

# No One Rejects
You but You

## The Prison of Guilt and Shame

It took me decades to forgive myself for surviving.

I graduated from college in 1969. I was forty-two years old, a mother of three, an immigrant. It had required significant courage and resources to learn English and return to school. And I was graduating with honors!

But I didn't go to my graduation ceremony. I was too ashamed.

Like many survivors, in the years after the war I'd grappled with crippling guilt. It had been twenty-four years since my sister Magda and I were liberated. But I still couldn't understand why I had lived when my parents and grandparents and six million others had perished. Even an occasion of celebration and accomplishment was tainted by my certainty that I was damaged goods, unworthy of joy, that every bad thing was somehow my fault, that it was only a matter of time before everyone discovered how broken I was.

Guilt is when you blame yourself, when you believe something is your fault. It's important to separate guilt from remorse.

Remorse is an appropriate response to a harmful mistake we've made or a wrong we've committed. It's more akin to grief. It means accepting that the past is the past, that it can't be undone, and allowing yourself to feel sad about it. I can feel remorse *and* recognize that all I've lived through, all the choices I've made, have brought me to today. Remorse is in the present. And it can coexist with forgiveness and freedom.

But guilt keeps you stuck. It's rooted in shame—when you believe "I'm not worthy"; when you think that you're not enough, that nothing is enough, no matter what you do. Guilt and shame can be extremely debilitating. But they're not real assessments of who we are. They're a pattern of thought that we choose and get stuck in.

You always have a choice about what to do with the information life hands you. I once gave a lecture at a conference, and midway through my presentation, a dignified-looking man walked out. I almost froze on the stage, caught up in a barrage of negative self-talk: "I'm no good. I don't deserve to have been invited to present at this conference. I'm out of my league." A few minutes later, the auditorium door opened, and the same man came back in and sat down. He'd probably just gotten up to have some water or use the restroom, but by that time I'd already put myself under the guillotine.

No one is born with shame. But for many of us, the shame message starts early. When Lindsey, my oldest grandchild, was in elementary school, she was placed in a class for "talented and gifted" children (the very notion of this label frustrates me—*all* children are talented and gifted, one-of-a-kind diamonds!). She sometimes had trouble keeping up, and her teacher began to call her "my little caboose." Precious Lindsey took her teacher's words to heart. She became convinced that she wasn't capable enough to be in the class, that she didn't belong, that she wasn't worthy. She was ready to drop out. But I talked to her about the importance of not letting her teacher define her. So she stayed in the class. And years later, when she wrote her college admittance essay, she titled it, "When the Caboose Became the Engine." She graduated with honors from Princeton.

My shame messages began early, too, at age three, when I became cross-eyed. Before I had surgery to correct my eye, my sisters would sing cruel songs: *you're so ugly and puny you'll never find a husband.* Even my mother would say, "It's a good thing you're smart, because you have no looks." These were difficult messages, and hard to unlearn. But ultimately the trouble wasn't what my family told me. The trouble was that I believed it.

And kept believing it.

When Marianne and Rob and their kids lived in La Jolla, I used to go to their house every Monday to cook dinner. Sometimes I made American food, sometimes Hungarian. It was the highlight of my week, nourishing my grandchildren, feeling a part of their daily lives. One evening I was in the kitchen with pots bubbling and pans sizzling on the stove. Marianne came home from work in her beautiful silk suit and immediately began pulling lids out of the cupboard, matching each one to the correct pot. My heart sank. I was trying to be helpful, to make my family happy, and there she was, showing me that I wasn't doing it right. That I wasn't good enough. It took me a while to realize that the message of my failure wasn't

> FREEDOM LIES IN ACCEPTING OUR WHOLE, IMPERFECT SELVES AND GIVING UP THE NEED FOR PERFECTION.

coming from Marianne—it was coming from me. To counteract my belief that I was damaged, I strove for perfection, believing I could achieve and perform my way out of shame. But we're human, no more, no less, and human means fallible. Freedom lies in accepting our whole, imperfect selves and giving up the need for perfection.

Ultimately, guilt and shame don't come from the outside. They come from the inside. Many of my patients seek out therapy when they're going through a painful divorce or breakup. They're grieving the death of a relationship, and the disappearance of all the hopes, dreams, and expectations it represented. But usually they don't talk about the grief—they talk about the feeling of rejection. "He rejected me." "She rejected me." But rejection is just a word we make up to express the feeling we have when we don't get what we want. Who said everyone should love us? Which god said that we should get what we want, when we want it, how we want it, the way we want it? And who said that having it all is any guarantee? No one rejects you but you.

So choose the meaning you make. When I give a speech and receive a standing ovation and embrace a hundred people afterward who greet me with tears and say, "You changed my life," and then one person shakes my hand and says, "Your talk was very good, *but* . . . ," I can choose how I respond. I can fall into a pit of insecurity, thinking, "Oh my god, what did I do wrong?" Or I can recognize that the critique might have more to do with the people offering it than with me—with the expectations they brought to the lecture, or with the way they feel strong and intelligent by finding something to criticize. Or I can ask myself, "Is there any-thing helpful here that can support my growth and creativity?" Whether I plan to integrate the feedback, or release it, I can say, "Thank you for your opinion" and move on.

If we're to live free of shame, we don't let others' evaluations define us.

And most of all, we choose how we talk to ourselves.

Spend a day listening to your self-talk. Pay attention to what you're paying attention to—that's what you reinforce. These thoughts will influence how you feel. And how you feel is going to dictate how you act. But you don't have to live by these stan-dards and messages. You weren't born with shame. Your genuine self is already beautiful. You were born with love and joy and passion, and you can rewrite your internal script and reclaim your innocence. You can become a whole person.

For as long as Michelle can remember, when people met her on the street they'd say, "I would give anything to be you." Tall, thin, beautiful, professionally successful, with a lovely, soft energy that people wanted to be near, she was picture-perfect on the outside—and dying inside.

Countless times I've seen this devastating dynamic in my practice: driven husband, wife who is a very good actress—the "hostess with the mostest." She's faultlessly kind and generous to others, but not a very good caretaker to herself. He's an actor, too, very loving and romantic when company is there, but in pri-vate, becoming more like her boss or parent, telling her what she should and shouldn't do, how she should spend her time and money. By pleasing, placating, and accommodating in reaction to the husband's dominance, the wife abdicates her adult power, lets him make all the decisions. And then gets even by depriving herself of food because it's the one thing she can control. She detaches from and minimizes her feelings of powerlessness by literally minimizing herself—making her body smaller and smaller. In the direst cases, even when she wants to start eating again, she can't. Her body rejects the nutrients.

Michelle had a very entrenched eating disorder by the time she began therapy (not with me—with a wonderful practitioner in her city). But it wasn't anorexia that drove her to seek help—it was problems in her marriage. Her husband was often dismissive and unkind, leaving her feeling like a scared kid with an angry dad. She knew rationally that she was a strong, successful, middle-aged woman, not a powerless child. But inside, she was terrified to stand up to him. When his outbursts of anger began to worry and frighten their children, she knew she needed new tools.

But learning to stand up for herself meant opening up her intense shame—all the pain she was trying to hold down by starving. When she started eating again—a process I always recommend doing under supervision of a medical doctor or in a specialized in- or outpatient program—all the trauma and feelings she'd tried to keep at bay rose up like a tidal wave. Childhood sexual abuse, a mother who was dismissive and emotionally cut off, parents who punished her with beatings, or worse, turned her invisible, not speaking to her at all, treating her as if she wasn't there. It was overwhelming to feel the terror and pain, to let the past in. She could only do it in small doses. She'd allow herself to feel, and then starve herself, allow herself to feel, then starve again.

The process brought up an excruciating fear of abandonment.

"I've always clung to the people I feel care about me, that see me, hear me, accept the real me," Michelle said. "When I was a kid, it was a teacher I felt safe with. As I got older, it was a professor, then my therapist. There's always a person I'm anxiously attached to. Logically, as an adult in my forties, I know I'm safe and cared for. Yet often I feel like that eight-year-old girl again, terrified that I'm going to lose love, terrified that I'm going to do something that'll make others not care about me."

Remember, you're the only one you'll never lose. You can look outside yourself to feel cherished—or you can learn to cherish yourself.

Three years since beginning therapy, Michelle has made tremendous progress. She's eating healthy foods in healthy portions. She's no longer exercising in excess. She's able to tell her husband when his criticism is hurtful, and use mindfulness techniques to ease the fear responses in her body. And she continues to work on releasing the shame she carries, shame that emerges in three harmful thought patterns: *it's my fault*, *I don't deserve it*, and *it could have been worse*.

She told me, "I keep thinking, 'Why didn't I do things differently?' Logically, I know it wasn't my fault, the things that happened to me, but there's a part of me that's still struggling with really believing it."

If you want to take charge of your thinking, first examine what you're practicing, and then decide: is it empowering or depleting me? Before you say anything, especially to yourself, ask, "Is it kind and loving?"

Michelle's childhood ended when the sexual and physical abuse began when she was eight, just at the age when our frontal lobes begin to develop, and we start to think logically. We want to understand things. But certain things we'll never understand. Sometimes we develop guilt in order to gain a sense of control over things that are completely out of our control, that we didn't cause or choose.

"Stop trying to find a reason for the abuse," I said, "and start practicing kindness. Pick an arrow that you follow."

"Ah, kindness," she said, letting out a low laugh. "Being kind to others has always come naturally. But being kind to myself is a struggle. At some level, I think I don't deserve the goodness in my life. I don't fully believe it's okay for me to be happy."

"You can say, 'That used to be me.' And regain power over your thinking. One word is all you need: permission. I give myself permission for pleasure.'"

She began to cry.

"Honey, take back your power."

But she was using minimization instead, telling herself things could be so much worse. Even though she got hit with a paddle, at least her parents didn't put cigarettes out on her arm, she'd tell herself.

I told her to get rid of the "shoulds." To make her language kinder. "Tune in to the way you speak to yourself," I said. "Acknowledge you were wounded. And then choose what you let go and what you replenish. You got in the habit of minimizing your pain, and wanting to make yourself smaller. Now build a new habit. Release shame by replacing it with kindness, by making sure your dialogue is full of 'yes I am, yes I can, yes I will!'"

\*     \*     \*

While visiting the Midwest once on a speaking tour, I was invited to eat dinner with a lovely family. The food was earthy and delicious, the conversation pleasant, but when I complimented the daughter, the mother kicked me under the table. Later, over coffee and dessert, she whispered, "Please

**FALL IN LOVE WITH YOURSELF! IT'S NOT NARCISSISTIC.**

don't lavish praise on her. I don't want her to grow up conceited." In trying to keep our children or ourselves modest, we risk making ourselves less than we really are—less than whole. It's time to give yourself a kiss on the hand and say, "Attaboy! Attagirl!"

Loving yourself is the only foundation for wholeness, health, and joy. So fall in love with yourself! It's not narcissistic. Once you begin to heal, what you discover will not be the *new* you, but the *real* you. The you that was there all along, beautiful, born with love and joy.

# KEYS TO FREE YOURSELF
# FROM GUILT AND SHAME

- *You made it.* If there's some part of yourself you routinely resent or criticize, imagine yourself being very little, so tiny you can crawl inside your body and say hello to each of your organs, to each part of yourself. If you believe that everything is your fault, then gently hold your heart, hug that wounded part of you, and exchange it for a loving self. Tell yourself, "Yes, I made a mistake. It doesn't make me a bad person. My doing is not the entirety of my being. I am good." If your trauma is still living in your body, embrace it, because you survived it. You're still here. You made it. My breathing has been very limited since my back broke during the war, so I like to go inside myself and say hello to my breathing, to my lungs. Find your vulnerable part and love it all over.

- *What you pay attention to grows stronger.* Spend a day listening to your self-talk. Is it full of "I should," "I shouldn't," and "yes, but"? Do you tell yourself, "It's my fault," or "I don't deserve it," or "It could have been worse"? Replace these messages of guilt or shame with a daily practice of kind and loving self-talk. As soon as you wake up in the morning, go to the mirror and look at yourself with loving eyes. Say, "I'm powerful. I'm kind. I'm a person of strength." Then kiss yourself on the back of each hand. Smile at yourself in the mirror. Say, "I love you."

# CHAPTER 6

# What Didn't Happen

# The Prison of Unresolved Grief

One day two women came to see me back-to-back. The first had a daughter who was a hemophiliac. She'd just come from the hospital, and she wept the whole hour, feeling the intense pain of watching her child suffer. My next patient had come from the country club. She also spent the hour weeping. She was upset because her new Cadillac had been delivered, and it had come in the wrong shade of yellow.

On the surface, her reaction seemed out of proportion, her tears unearned. But often a minor disappointment represents a larger grief. Her sense of loss wasn't about the Cadillac—it was about her relationships with her husband and son, the sorrow and resentment she felt that her desires for her family went unmet.

These two beautiful women reminded me of one of the most fundamental principles of my work: how it is a universal experience for life not to turn out as we want or expect. Most of us suffer because we have something we don't want, or we want something we don't have.

All therapy is grief work. A process of confronting a life where you expect one thing and get another, a life that brings you the unexpected and unanticipated.

This is the epitome of what most soldiers face in combat. I've worked with many combat veterans throughout my career, and they often tell me the same thing: that they were sent to a place they were unprepared for, and that they were told one thing and found another.

Grief is often not about what happened. It's about what didn't happen. When Marianne went to her first high school prom in a gorgeous orange silk dress, Béla told her, "Have fun, honey. When your mother was your age she was in Auschwitz and her parents were dead." I was speechless with fury. My children knew by then that I was a survivor, but how dare he burden our precious daughter with my past? How dare he ruin her night with something that had nothing to do with her? It was completely unfair. Totally inappropriate.

**REGRET IS THE WISH TO CHANGE THE PAST.**

But I was also so upset because he was right. I never got to put on an orange silk dress and go to a dance. Hitler interrupted my life, and the lives of millions of others.

I'm a prisoner and a victim when I minimize or deny my pain—and I'm a prisoner and a victim when I hold on to regret. Regret is the wish to change the past. It's what we experience when we can't acknowledge that we're powerless, that something already happened, that we can't change a single thing.

\*       \*       \*

I wish my mother had had a better guide through a sudden loss when she was nine. She woke up to find that her mother, who slept beside her, had stopped breathing, her body gone cold in the night. They buried her that day. There was no time to mourn, and all the years I knew her, my mother struggled with unresolved grief. She immediately took on the responsibility of caring for her younger siblings and cooking for the family, watching her father turn to alcohol to dull his pain and loneliness. By the time she married and became a mother herself, her grief had calcified, the shock and sorrow of her early loss tight around her like a cage. She hung a portrait of her mother on the wall above the piano and talked to it as she went about her chores. In the soundtrack of my childhood, my sister Klara practices violin, and my mother begs her dead mother for help and strength. Her grief seemed like a fourth child, in need of constant tending. It's good to feel all the aspects of grief—sadness, anger, powerlessness. But my mother got stuck there.

When we have unresolved grief, we often live with overwhelming rage.

Lorna had a brother who drank a lot. One night he went for a walk and was hit by a car and died. A year later, she is struggling to accept that he's gone. "I told him and told him not to drink!" she says. "Why didn't he listen? He was supposed to help me take care of our mother. How could he be so selfish?" She can't change that he was addicted to alcohol, that he kept right on drinking despite his family's best efforts to intervene, that he was inebriated when he died. She can't change a thing—and it's hard to accept our powerlessness.

When my grandchildren were young, a schoolmate was riding his bike one afternoon when he cut in front of traffic and died. Marianne was asked to talk to his classmates, to help them process all the complex feelings that come with loss—the way it forces us into a reckoning with our own mortality, with the fragility of life. She came prepared to address their sadness and fear. But the students' overwhelming response to the tragedy wasn't sorrow. It was guilt. "I could have been nicer to him," they said. "He could have been at my house instead of riding his bike alone, but I never wanted to invite him over." The students enumerated all the ways they might have prevented the boy's death. By holding themselves responsible, they were seeking control. But as long as they continued to blame themselves, they'd be avoiding their grief.

We don't have control, but we wish we did.

Resolving grief means both to release ourselves from responsibility for all the things that weren't up to us, and to come to terms with the choices we've made that can't be undone.

Marianne helped the children name all the decisions that weren't in their control: the boy's choice to ride his bike that day, the route he took, what he was or wasn't paying attention to when he rode off the curb into the street, what the driver of the car was or wasn't paying attention to as she moved into the intersection. And she helped them face their remorse for choices they *had* made: the sleepovers and birthday parties they hadn't invited the boy, the teasing remarks, the times they'd laughed or stayed silent when he was the butt of a prank. This is the work we get to do in the present: to grieve what happened or didn't happen, to own up to what we did or didn't do, and to choose our response now. Being more attuned to how their behavior might hurt or marginalize others wasn't going to bring their classmate back. But they could embrace the opportunity to become more aware—to act with greater kindness and compassion.

It's so hard to be where we are, in the present. To accept what was and is, and move on. For twenty years, my patient Sue has come to see me every year around the anniversary of her son's death. When he was twenty-five, he shot himself with the gun she kept in her bedside table. He's been dead now almost as long as he was alive, and she's still healing, still trapped sometimes in the unrelenting eddy of guilt. *Why did I own a gun? Why didn't I secure it properly? Why did I allow him to find it? Why was I so unaware of his depression and troubles?* She can't seem to forgive herself.

Of course, she wishes he hadn't died. She longs to erase all the factors, large and small, that may have contributed to his death. But her son didn't end his life because she owned a gun. He didn't kill himself because of anything she did or didn't do.

But as long as she stays in guilt, she doesn't have to acknowledge that he died. As long as she can blame herself, she doesn't have to accept what *he* chose to do. If he could see her suffering now, he would probably say, "Mom, I was going to kill myself anyway. I didn't want you to die with me."

It's good to keep crying for those we've lost, to keep feeling the ache, to let ourselves be in the sorrow and accept that it's not ever going to go away. I was invited to speak at a support group for grieving parents where they shared memories and pictures, cried together, showed up for each other. It was beautiful to witness this connected and supportive way of living grief.

I also noticed some ways I could guide them toward greater freedom within their grief. For example, they began the meeting by going around in a circle and introducing themselves and the child who had died. "I lost my daughter to suicide," one said;

another, "I lost my son when he was two." Each person used the verb "lost" in describing his or her grief.

"But life is not about lost and found," I told them.

It's about celebrating that the spirits of our loved ones came to us—sometimes for a few short days, sometimes for many decades—and it's about letting go. About acknowledging the sorrow and joy that coexist in this moment, and embracing all of it.

Parents often say, "I'd die for my child." I heard a few of the parents in the grief group express the wish to trade places with their deceased children—to die so their children could live. After the war, I felt the same way. I would have gladly died to bring my parents and grandparents back.

But now I know that instead of dying for my dead, I can *live* for them.

And live for my children and grandchildren and great-grandchildren—for all my loved ones who are still here.

If we can't move on from our guilt and make peace with our grief, it's damaging to our loved ones, and not a compliment to those who've died. We have to let the dead be dead, to stop yanking them up again and again, to let them go and to live our own best lives so they can rest in peace.

Sofia is at a critical place in her grief.

Her mother was a dynamic teacher and celebrated psychologist who finished her master's degree at age fifty (like me!) and became certified in Viktor Frankl's logotherapy (like me!)—a theory and method of guiding patients to discover meaning in their lives and experience. She was still working at age seventy, and had just published her first book, when she started having back pain. She was an exceptionally healthy woman—Sofia can't remember her ever having so much as a cold—but suddenly she was refusing food, avoiding family events and social functions because her back hurt so intensely. She saw a specialist who found nothing wrong. She went from specialist to specialist, trying to discover the root of the pain, and finally a gastroenterologist performed the tests that revealed her diagnosis: stage-four pancreatic cancer. She died a month later.

For a year, Sofia was in constant mourning, crying all the time. The passage of time has dulled her intense shock and sadness, and the pain is less raw and consuming—but she's in a precarious place, a crossroads where she can choose to heal or stay stuck. To heal doesn't mean to get over it, but it does mean that we are able to be wounded and whole, to find happiness and fulfillment in our lives despite our loss.

"She died so suddenly," Sofia told me. "There was no time to prepare, and I have so many regrets."

"Do you have guilt? Do you think there's something you could have done that you didn't do?"

"Yes," she said. "My mom was so strong, I never thought she was dying. I scolded her for not eating. I was trying to help her, but if I'd known they were her last days, I would have reacted differently."

She was imprisoned by two words: what if. *What if I'd known she was dying? What if I'd known I was about to lose her?* But what-ifs don't empower us. They deplete us.

I told Sofia, "Today you can say, 'If I knew then what I know now, I would have done things differently.' And that's the end of the guilt. Because you owe it to your mom to turn that guilt around. Just say, 'That used to be me. Now I will begin to cherish the memories that no one can take away.' You had her for thirty-four wonderful years. There will never be another mom like that. There will never be another therapist like that. So cherish the person she was and the time you had, and don't waste another moment on guilt, because guilt does not produce love. Ever."

Guilt stops us from enjoying our memories. And it prevents us from living fully now.

"When you're guilty, you're not available to be playful, to have intimacy," I told Sofia. "And you're tarnishing the beautiful things. The memory of blow-drying your mom's hair in the hospital, helping her feel elegant and pretty as she wished to be in her final days. The gift that she went quickly, without suffering for years and years, unable to control her faculties."

Sometimes we may feel that we're cheating on the dead if we laugh too much, that we're abandoning them if we have too much fun, forgetting them if we're happy.

"But you belong dancing with your husband," I said, "not sitting at home crying for your mom. So get rid of that punitive parent voice in you—the *should've, could've, why didn't I.* You're not free when you're guilty. If your mom were sitting with you now, what would she tell you she wishes for you?"

"For my sisters and me to be happy. For us to live a full life."

"And you can give her that gift. Have a full life. Celebrate. Your whole life is ahead of you now. I see her winking at you, encouraging you. So show up for your sisters and your husband. Love each other. And when you're ninety-two you can think of me, and how your life began when your precious mother died and you made the decision to have a full life, and not be a victim of any circumstance. It's your job now to give her a gift: let go. Let go."

\*      \*      \*

Grief has so many layers and flavors: sorrow, fear, relief, survivor's guilt, existential questioning, diminished safety, fragility. Our whole sense of the world is interrupted and rearranged. The adage says, "Time heals all wounds." But I disagree. Time doesn't heal. It's what you do with the time.

Sometimes people compensate for the upheaval of grief by trying to keep everything the same—jobs, routines, and relationships remain static. But when you've had a big loss, nothing is the same anymore. Grief can be an invitation to revisit our priorities and decide again—to reconnect to our joy and purpose, recommit to being the best we can be right now, to embrace that life is pointing us in a new direction.

**GRIEF CAN BE AN INVITATION TO REVISIT OUR PRIORITIES.**

When grief came knocking—which it does, to you, to me, to everyone—Daniel wasn't content to live automatically, doing the same thing over and over. He was ready to switch gears and take back his power.

As he put it, "Something so hard or tragic can happen that a person has to make a choice to continue being the same way, or make a change for the better."

His story of loss began as a love story. He met Tracy when he was eighteen years old. Both indigenous Canadians, they were studying the same subjects—environmental science and indigenous studies—at university. Right away they became good conversationalists and good friends, talking for hours at a stretch, relaxed and happy in each other's company.

But now Daniel reflects, "There was a lot we didn't talk about that we probably should have."

Daniel was twenty-five when they married, thirty when their son, Joseph, was born. They moved across the country to Tracy's home province. That's when things began to sour. She was thriving academically and professionally—she finished her master's degree and started working on her doctorate, and was a respected environmental expert and sought-after consultant. But being back at home underscored all the reasons she'd left in the first place: rampant alcoholism and drug addiction in the community, as well as violence and deaths. And, though Daniel didn't know it yet, she was again in proximity to tragic abuse that had occurred within her own family. She fell into a tailspin, often drinking and raging, and she and Daniel separated. Joseph was just two.

They did their best to coparent in a respectful way, sharing custody fifty-fifty, managing not to fight around their son. But Tracy's life was growing more tumultuous. Her driver's license was suspended, he presumes for drunk driving, and on several occasions when Daniel dropped Joseph off, he felt uneasy, a fleeting sense that she might be high. He confronted her about his concerns, and she said she was dealing with difficult personal issues, but had it under control.

Once, concerned for her welfare, Daniel left Joseph at home with a babysitter and went looking for her. He found her at a relative's house, sleeping off a hangover. When she woke up, she seemed distraught. He sat on the bed with her. Sobbing, she revealed that when she was twelve she'd been sexually abused by members of her own family. At age eighteen, she'd confronted her parents, and her mother sat tightlipped and rigidly silent while her father threw it back in her face, blaming her for what had happened. Daniel was shocked. He knew she'd had it rough as a kid, that she and her siblings had been beaten. But he'd had no idea about the sexual abuse. It helped him understand how much she was hurting—and it ignited a new set of concerns. He told her, "From now on I can't have Joseph around anyone who does that to a child. So that's the new rule. No contact with your parents until this is brought out and talked about." She agreed. But a month later she filed for divorce. And a year later she gave their son to her father to watch. When Daniel found out, he took her to court and earned full custody.

With Tracy's blessing, Daniel moved to be closer to his family. They planned for Tracy to move, too, to be near Joseph and far away from the chaos of abuse and addiction at home. In the meantime, Daniel regularly drove Joseph to visit her, and she sometimes traveled to see them. She seemed a ghost of herself—deep shadows under her eyes, her body somehow lethargic yet agitated. But when Daniel expressed concern, she was dismissive, face taut and eyes vacant.

And then she went missing.

No one knows the exact day she disappeared. Some say she had been in the company of a drug dealer. Joseph was five the last time he saw his mother.

"It was shocking," Daniel told me. "Mind-boggling. She was an accomplished woman. Her community looked to her for help in the environmental field. I'd always known her to be a great person. When I look back at it now, I guess all those things were lying buried, never dealt with, catching up."

He'd been grieving already—for the loss of his best friend as a life partner, the loss of their marriage, the loss of his coparent. But now the grief was absolute—and ominous. Tracy was gone all of a sudden, and forever. No one would likely ever know why. She'd become one of countless missing and murdered indigenous women in the United States and Canada, where indigenous women face murder rates as much as ten times the national average.

Daniel felt like he was spinning through a revolving door, recounting all the ways he'd failed her—every hurtful thing he'd ever said or done or been a part of, all the ways he'd missed understanding just how alone and out of place she must have felt in the world. He was surprised to find that her disappearance stirred up his own older grief, things he didn't realize were still festering inside, unhealed—the ways he hadn't known or accepted himself as a child, the onslaught of racism he'd experienced in school, the years he'd spent hating himself and contemplating suicide, the trouble he'd always had communicating his desires and boundaries. He'd been taught to be tough, to carry on, isolate, shut down his feelings, all in the guise of moving forward and onward. It was the same now. Well-intentioned people told him to toughen up and be a man, that she was in a better place now, that God had a plan.

These things may be true. "But they don't help you get the pain and turmoil out of your body," he said.

For three years, grief pushed him to his knees and held him underground.

"I could work and laugh and function," he said, "but I was on cruise control a lot of the time." If something triggered him, the bad feeling would last for days or weeks. Saddest of all, he knew he had no tools to help Joseph work through his emotions.

There didn't seem to be a way out. He consciously accepted that he would be depressed and unhappy the rest of his life.

But what he was willing to accept for himself, he couldn't accept for his son. His love for Joseph was his saving grace, the catalyst that allowed change to come about.

In order to better guide his son, Daniel started reading about grief. Reading led to talking. He started therapy, and in doing his own grief work, he found a new professional calling, completing a grief-therapy certification program and envisioning the life he wanted, unwaveringly repeating and believing it would happen, even if he didn't know how.

Now Daniel works with Child and Family Services and also runs boys' grief groups in the public schools, counseling troubled children and teens, many of whom have been in care since they were two or three. He says that a lot of grief work is about being quiet—about holding space. Sometimes he and the boys go for walks, or build a fire outside, or sit in silence at McDonald's.

"My career keeps me practicing," he said. "Helping others through the forest I walked through, I'm always reflecting, doing my own constant tending, keeping Tracy in my heart, staying aware of where I am and how I'm doing."

In my experience, grief brings us together—or it pushes us apart. Either way, we're never the same. Daniel is a beautiful example of how it's possible for grief to guide us in a positive direction.

And his story reminds us that grief isn't something you only do once. Grief will always be a part of their lives and relationship. And as Joseph grows and matures, Daniel will have to figure out all over again how to talk to him about his mother. There will always be questions with no answers.

\*    \*    \*

Some things you'll never understand. Don't even try to.

There are so many reasons why—why this or that happened, or didn't; why we are where we are; why we do what we do. Grief forces us to get clear about what's my business, what's your business, and what's God's business.

When the kapo at Auschwitz pointed at the smoke rising from the crematorium and said, "You can start talking about your mother in the past tense. She's already dead," my sister Magda told me, "The spirit never dies." She's right. When I go and speak at a school, I'm doing it out of love for my parents, so I can keep their memories alive, to learn from the past so we don't repeat it.

And I talk to my parents. Not in the bereft way my mother called on her mother for help. But to cultivate the place in my heart where their spirits still live. To call them to witness how rich and full my life is—to see what they allowed to grow and thrive in the world.

I inherited my father's taste for fashion and couture, and every time I get dressed, I say to him, "Papa, look at me! You always said I was going to be the best-dressed girl in town." When I put myself together well, when I feel that contentment and chutzpah, it's a ritual of celebration for my father.

To my mother, I offer thanks. For her wisdom, for how she taught me to find the power within. I even thank her for the times she told me, "I'm glad you have brains, because you have no looks"! Thank you, Mama, for doing the best with what you had. Thank you for the strength you had to take care of your drunk, grief-stricken father, to feed and nourish your family and ours. Thank you for inspiring me to discover my inner resources. I love you. I'll never forget you.

Grieving is difficult, but it can also feel good. You can revisit the past. You can even embrace it. You're not stuck there. You're here now. And you're strong.

You can come to terms with what was and what wasn't. And you can concentrate not on what you lost, but on what is left: the choice to live every moment as a gift, to embrace what *is*.

# KEYS TO FREE YOURSELF FROM UNRESOLVED GRIEF

- **Let the dead be dead.** *Grief changes, but it doesn't go away. Denying your grief won't help you heal—nor will it help to spend more time with the dead than you do with the living. If someone you love has died, give yourself thirty minutes every day to honor the person and the loss. Take an imaginary key, unlock your heart, and free your grief. Cry, yell, listen to music that reminds you of your loved one, look at pictures, read old letters. Express and be with your grief, 100 percent. When the thirty minutes have passed, tuck your loved one safely inside your heart and get back to living.*

- **The spirit never dies.** *It's possible for grief to guide us in a positive direction, toward a life with more joy and meaning and purpose. Talk to the loved one who has passed. Say what you're thankful for: the memories you cherish, the skills he or she taught you, the gifts you carry with you because that person touched your life. Then ask, "What do you wish for me?"*

# CHAPTER 7

# Nothing
to Prove

# The Prison of Rigidity

When a couple tells me they never fight, I say, "Then you don't have intimacy, either."

Conflict is human. When we avoid conflict, we're actually moving closer to tyranny than to peace. Conflict itself isn't imprisoning. What keeps us trapped is the rigid thinking we often use to manage conflict.

The prison bars of rigid thinking can be hard to recognize because they're often gilded in good intentions. Many people seek me out for therapy because they want to improve their relationships—to find a better way to communicate with their partners or children, to have more peace and intimacy. But often I discover that they're not in therapy to learn how to negotiate conflict; they want my help in convincing others to conform to their point of view. If you come in with an agenda, if you're keeping score or trying to change someone else, then you're not free. Freedom is when you embrace your power to choose your own response.

My patients say it all the time: "I want him to . . ." or, "I want her to . . ." But you can't want something for another person. You can only discover what's right *for you*.

This is one of the most important tools for managing conflict: stop denying someone else's truth. I love a good tongue sandwich. But my friend says, "How can you eat that? I get sick just thinking about it." So who's right? He's right for him, and I'm right for me. You don't have to agree. You don't have to give up your truth—and please don't ever do that! Freedom comes in letting go of the need to be right.

When I realized decades after the war that in order to heal I had to go back to Auschwitz and face the past, I invited my sister Magda to come with me. We had kept each other alive when we were prisoners; we had been each other's reason to live. I wanted to go back with her to the place where our parents were murdered. To face what happened, to grieve, to be at the site of constant terror and death and say, "We made it!" But she thought I was an idiot. Who would willingly return to hell? My sister, the only person on the planet who shared so much with me, the person to whom I credit my very survival, had a completely different response to our common experience. And neither one of us is wrong or right, better or worse, healthier or unhealthier. I'm right for Edie, Magda's right for Magda. We are both human—beautiful and fallible, no more, no less. And we're both right. I went back to Auschwitz alone.

This is what I think Jesus meant when he advised us to "turn the other cheek." When you turn the other cheek, you look at the same thing from a new perspective. You can't change the situation, you can't change someone else's mind, but you can look at reality differently. You can accept and integrate multiple points of view. This flexibility is our strength.

It's what allows us to be assertive—not aggressive or passive or passive-aggressive. When we're aggressive, we decide for others. When we're passive, we let others decide for us. And when we're passive-aggressive, we prevent others from deciding for themselves. When you're assertive, you speak in statements. When I wanted to go back to school, I was afraid of Béla's opinion, afraid he would resent my time away from the family, afraid he wouldn't like us being introduced as "Dr. and Mr. Eger." But when you're a whole person, an adult, you don't have to ask anyone's permission. So don't put your life in someone else's hands. Just make a statement: "I've decided to go back to school and get my doctorate." Give the other person the information and freedom they need to be assertive about their wants and hopes and fears.

The key to maintaining your freedom during a conflict is to hold your truth while also relinquishing the need for power and control.

It helps when we can meet others as they are, not as we expect them to be. I have a patient who is often in conflict with his teenage daughter. One session, he was upset because when they'd escalated into a fight about whether or not she could use the car, his daughter blew up at him, calling him names and using profanity. He wanted me to be the judge, to hear the evidence and pronounce his daughter guilty, to take his side. But we don't empower others—or ourselves—when we launch into complaints, when we say here's-what-you-did this, here's-what-you-did that. No one grows with criticism. So eliminate it. No criticism. None, ever.

**NO ONE GROWS WITH CRITICISM.**

We do this for others, but most of all for ourselves, so we can live free of unrealistic expectations, and free of the anger that comes when our expectations are not met. I'm very selective about who's going to get my anger, because when I'm angry, I'm the one who suffers.

Unhealthy conflict has everything to do with being locked in a better-than, less-than mind-set. When Béla and I were traveling in Europe one summer, we discovered that the Bolshoi Ballet tour was scheduled to come through Paris while we were there. I'd always dreamed of seeing them perform. Béla bought me a ticket and dropped me off at the theater, but wouldn't go inside. I thought it was about the money—that he didn't want to spend more on a second ticket. I came out at intermission, entranced by the performance, and encouraged him to come in for the second half. "There are open seats," I said. "Get a ticket and come enjoy this with me." But he wouldn't go in. "I don't give money to Russians," he said. "Not after what the Communists did to me in Czechoslovakia." He'd convinced himself that this was how he could avenge the cruelties and imprisonment he'd suffered. I argued with him, urged him to reconsider, told him, "These artists have nothing to do with what happened to you." But of course I couldn't change his mind. I went back into the theater and enjoyed the rest of the performance, for me. On one hand, it's too bad he couldn't set aside his judgment and anger, and sit with me in the dark, enjoying something breathtakingly beautiful. On the other hand, I can't say my way was better than his way. Béla's way was better for Béla, my way was better for me.

Many of us live as though we have something to prove. We can become addicted to having the last word. But if you're trying to prove that you're right or you're good, you're trying to make yourself into something that doesn't exist. Every human is fallible. Every human makes mistakes. You're not helpless—and you're not a saint, either. You don't have to prove your worth. You can just embrace it, celebrate that you're imperfect and whole, that there will never be another you. Drop the agenda. If you have something to prove, you're still a prisoner.

This is even true in the face of someone else's unkindness or persecution.

My friend's daughter came home from kindergarten very upset because her classmate had called her "poopy-face." My friend asked me how she could help her daughter deal with the conflict. It's important that we give up the need to defend ourselves. We're all probably going to face bullies. But if someone calls you a poopy-face, don't say, "I'm not a poopy-face!" Don't defend yourself against a crime you never committed. It just becomes a power struggle. The bully throws you a rope, you pick up the other end, and you're both tugging and exhausted. It takes two to fight. But it takes one to stop. So don't pick up the rope. Tell yourself, "The more he talks, the more relaxed I become." And remind yourself that it's not personal. When someone calls you "poopy-face" he's really talking about how he sees himself.

**IF YOU HAVE SOMETHING TO PROVE, YOU'RE STILL A PRISONER.**

I lectured once at the Satyagraha House in Johannesburg—a home where Mohandas Gandhi once lived, now a museum and retreat center. He was able to bring the British Empire to its knees, without any bloodshed, without the rhetoric of hate.

This is one of the ways I was able to survive Auschwitz. I was surrounded every moment by dehumanizing words—you're worthless, you're dirty, the only way you'll leave this place is as a corpse. But I didn't let the words penetrate my spirit.

Somehow I was blessed with the insight that the Nazis were more imprisoned than I was. I first understood this the night I danced for Mengele. My physical body was trapped in a death camp, but my spirit was free. Mengele and the others would always have to reckon with what they'd done. I was numb with shock and hunger, I was terrified of being murdered, but I still had an inner sanctuary. The Nazis' power came from systematic dehumanization and extermination. My strength and freedom were within.

Joy is a wonderful role model for how to dissolve rigid thinking. For many years, she was married to an abusive man. He treated her with disdain and contempt, hurting her verbally and financially, regularly threatening her with a gun to her head. She survived by keeping journals, meticulously cataloguing their interactions, what each of them said and did. It was a bid for sanity—keeping track of the truth day by day.

When I work with a patient who is in an abusive relationship, I always say: If your partner ever hits you, leave right away. Go to a transitional living center. Stay with a friend or relative. Take the kids, ask for help, and get out.

If you don't leave the first time, the abuser isn't going to take you seriously. And each instance of abuse will make it harder and harder to leave. The violence will usually get worse the longer you stay. And it will get more difficult to reverse the psychological aspects of the abuse, the things the abuser wants you to believe—that you're nothing without him, that when he hits you, it's your fault. Every minute you stay, you're putting yourself in harm's way. You are much too precious for that!

When someone hits you, it's an instant wake-up call. You know what you're dealing with. It isn't easy to leave, but once you have the awareness of your partner's capacity and tendency for violence, the problem is 50 percent solved. When the abuse is more covert and psychological, you may doubt what you see. You may ask, "Is this *really* happening to me?" If someone physically harms you, you know. Yes, it's happening. Yes, I've got to go.

Without the physical scars of abuse, it was difficult for Joy to leave the relationship. (This is another common experience for people trapped in an abusive dynamic—the fear, and too often the reality, that we won't be believed.) Eventually, realizing it was only a matter of time before her husband acted on his threats, Joy divorced him, and he slowly drank himself to death.

After he died, anger boiled through her. She had been clinging to the hope that one day he might apologize for the years of unkindness—recognize his mistakes, admit she was right to have left him. When he died, she had to accept that she'd never get an apology. She'd never get to win the fight. In an effort to make peace with the past, she went back to the journals she'd kept. What she read shocked her—not how cruel her husband had been, but how cruel she had been to him.

"I bullied my husband," she said. "I was thinking, 'He's abusing me,' but I was doing it right back to him. Keeping the kids from him, denying him things, using the kids as tools to get to him, just because I wanted to hurt him. I was so desperate. I thought there was no other way out. I couldn't see beyond the terrible situation. But he wasn't the only one making trouble in our marriage. I was, too."

Many volatile relationships are complicated. While nothing excuses domestic violence or abuse, there often isn't a right person and a wrong person, a good spouse and a bad spouse. Both partners are contaminating the relationship.

When I met Alison, she'd been divorced for twelve years. Sean, her ex, had entered her life shortly after the end of a tumultuous relationship with a guy who split her lip open during a fight, and then, when she left him, broke into her house and slashed her mattress apart with a knife. Sean swooped in like a savior—a caretaker and cheerleader who helped her feel safe and also helped launch her singing career, managing her tours and recording contracts, setting her up with master classes and performances with legendary musicians.

Though generous and caring, Sean could also be controlling. Alison relied on him, yet resented him for being in charge of her life, and she began to retaliate, vying for control by starving herself. She was hospitalized three times for an eating disorder, but the self-harm only escalated. When she began burning herself on the arm and leg, Sean lost hope. He had an affair, and then another, and eventually ended their eighteen-year marriage.

More than a decade later, Alison was still fighting with him. Over intellectual property rights to the songs they'd written together. Over his unfortunate attempt to seduce the student she'd sent to him for professional advice. Their marriage had ended long ago, but they were still locked in a power struggle, both making harmful choices.

I told Alison if she wanted to bring an end to the hostilities, she needed to look not at the causes of the conflict, but at the maintainers.

"How are you maintaining a point of view that isn't serving you anymore?" I asked.

Alison was preoccupied by the desire to prove Sean's guilt and her innocence. She essentially had him on trial in her mind, her inner life an ongoing courtroom drama. But it was an unwinnable fight.

"Honey," I told her, "you can be dead right—and you're still dead. So do you want to be happy, or do you want to be right?"

The best way to let go of the need for control is to become *powerful*. Power has nothing to do with brawn or domination. It means you have the strength to respond instead of react, to take charge of your life, to have total ownership of your choices. You are powerful because you're not giving your power away.

If you take back your power and *still* want to be right, then choose to be kind, because kindness is always right.

Limbering up our thinking can not only alter our relationship, but change our perceptions, the way we see and feel in the world.

As Alison began to free herself from the prison of rigidity, she was able to draw clearer boundaries with her ex and find renewed agency in her career, and she began planning an international tour. But then two physical challenges emerged suddenly and disturbed her hard-won peace. She developed a severe vocal tremor that made singing a challenge and threatened her career; and she injured her back. It hurt to go about her daily activities, and the things she did for fun and self-care—gardening, yoga—were unavailable until she healed. Her face was drawn into a stiff grimace, and I could hear her pain in the jagged way she spoke.

"I was doing so well," she said. "And now I'll probably have to cancel my tour."

Life isn't fair. And when we're hurting, our anger, worry, and frustration are completely legitimate. But we can face any circumstance, however unpleasant or unjust, with rigidity or flexibility.

"When your body hurts," I told her, "don't punish it, or resent it, or demand things of it. Say, 'I'm listening.'"

Alison developed a practice to move from rigidity to flexibility. She started with a statement of the problem, not minimizing or denying her pain or frustration.

"I don't like it," she said. "It hurts. It's inconvenient."

Then she stopped resisting and resenting her body, and started listening. She became curious.

"What do you want to tell me?" she asked. "What's in my best interest? What serves and empowers me now?"

For a while, her body told her the same thing: slow down. Rest. So she listened, and eventually her back began to improve. She was able to try a restorative yoga class. Back on the mat, she found that she was able to move more gently and mindfully now that she was less preoccupied with pushing herself and more attuned to her inner experience. Her definition of "getting it right" had changed. Before she hurt her back, she had something to prove—how long she could hold a difficult arm balance, how deeply she could twist. Now she was less imprisoned by expectations.

We don't have to like the difficult or painful things that happen to us. But when we stop fighting and resisting, we have more energy and imagination to move forward, instead of nowhere.

Joy discovered this, too. Like Alison, she'd been stuck in the prison of rigid thinking for years after her divorce, trapped in the mind-set of dichotomies: good/bad, right/wrong, victim/victimizer. Because she saw things in such stark and absolute terms, the stakes were always high—all or nothing, life or death, with nothing in between. This made any conflict, even a minor dispute, feel treacherous. Because there was no room in her mind-set for nuance or complexity, Joy couldn't bear for anyone to disagree with her.

"They might as well be pointing at me and saying, 'You're fat, you're ugly, you're worthless,'" she said.

When she discovered a more complex truth—that she had also been culpable in her marriage, that she wasn't always right—something remarkable happened. Her vision seemed to change. She could perceive colors more intensely. Freed from her black-and-white thinking and rigid interpretation of the past, the world appeared more vivid and vibrant. She drove her children crazy, pointing at flowers—yellow, red, purple, blue—saying, "Look at that! Look! Look!"

Flexibility is strength. I learned it when I was training as a gymnast, and it's why I go swing dancing as often as my body can handle, why I end each speech with a high kick.

And it's true for the psyche as well as for the body. You're strong when you're supple and limber. So get up each morning and stretch. Develop the mental range of motion that keeps you free.

# KEYS TO FREE YOURSELF FROM RIGIDITY

- *Give a gentle embrace.* *Choose a current challenge in your life—an injury or physical ailment, an ongoing tension or conflict, or any circumstance that has you feeling restricted, limited, or confined. Start by speaking your truth. What don't you like about it? How does it make you feel? Then get curious. Ask, "What is this situation telling me? What's in my best interest? What serves and empowers me now?"*

- *Meet others as they are.* *Write down the name of a person with whom you're in conflict. Then write all your complaints about this person. For example:* My daughter is rude and ungrateful. She calls me names and uses toxic language. She has no respect for me. She flat-out ignores me and breaks curfew. *Now, rewrite the list; this time, state what you observe, without any editorializing, interpretation, judgment, or assumptions. Eliminate rigid words like "always" and "never." Simply state the facts:* Sometimes my daughter raises her voice and uses swear words. Once or twice a week, she comes home later than 11:00 p.m.

- *Cooperation, not domination.* *Choose one thing from your list of observations that you'd like to address with the other person. Find a neutral time to talk—not in the heat of conflict. First, say what you notice: "I've noticed that a couple of times a week you come home later than*

11:00 p.m." Then, get curious about the other person's point of view. A simple question works best: "What's up?" Next, without blaming or shaming the other person, say what you want: "It's important to me that you get enough sleep during the week. And I'd like to know that you're home safe before I go to bed." Finally, invite the person to collaborate on a plan: "What ideas do you have for a solution that works for both of us?" It's okay if the conflict isn't resolved right away. The important thing is to shift into a cooperative way of addressing conflict—to privilege the relationship over either person's need for power and control.

- **Treat others as they are capable of becoming.** Visualize a person with whom you're experiencing conflict. Now envision this person's highest self. It might help to close your eyes and picture the person surrounded by light. Put your hand over your heart. Say, "I see you."

# CHAPTER 8

# Would You Like to Be Married to You?

## The Prison of Resentment

The biggest disruptor of intimacy is low-level, chronic anger and irritation.

My resentment toward Béla—for his impatience and temper, for the ways he remained stuck in the past, for the disappointment that sometimes showed in his face when he looked at our son—festered for so many years that I thought the only way to be free was to divorce him. It was only after we'd split, and completely disrupted our children's lives, not to mention our own, that I realized my disappointment and anger had little to do with Béla—and everything to do with me, with my own unfinished emotional business and unresolved grief.

The suffocation I felt in our marriage wasn't Béla's fault; it was the price of all the years I'd spent disowning my feelings: sorrow for my mother, who gave up an independent, cosmopolitan life working for a consulate in Budapest, and gave up a man she loved but was forbidden to marry because he wasn't

Jewish, to do what others expected her to do. Fear of repeating the loneliness of my parents' marriage. Grief over my first love, Eric, who died in Auschwitz. And grief for my parents. I got married and became a mother before I'd come to terms with my losses. And suddenly I was forty, the age my mother had been when she died. It felt like I was running out of time to live how I wanted to live: free. But instead of finding freedom by discovering my own genuine purpose and direction, I decided that freedom meant being away from Béla's yelling, cynicism, irritation, and disappointment—from the things I imagined limited me.

When we're angry, it's often because there's a gap between our expectations and reality. We think it's the other person who's trapping and aggravating us—but the real prison is our unrealistic expectations. Often, we marry like Romeo and Juliet, without really knowing each other. We fall in love with love, or with an image of a person to whom we've assigned all the traits and characteristics we crave, or with someone with whom we can repeat the familiar patterns we learned in our families of origin. Or we present a false self, seeking love and a secure relationship by giving up who we really are. Falling in love is a chemical high. It feels amazing—and it's temporary. When the feeling fades, we're left with a lost dream, with a sense of loss over the partner or relationship we never had in the first place. So many salvageable relationships are abandoned in despair.

But love isn't what you feel. It's what you do.

There's no going back to the early days of a relationship, to the time before you became angry and disappointed and cut off. There's something better: a renaissance. A new beginning.

*   *   *

Marina, a dancer and performance artist, was trying to figure out if such a rebirth was possible in her marriage—whether she and her husband could move forward together in a healthy way, or if the way to freedom meant finally letting go of the relationship.

"We've been fighting every day for eighteen years," she told me, twisting her long hair into a loose bun. Sometimes the fights were violent. Her husband didn't hit her, but he acted out—shoved chairs, threw his phone against the wall, overturned the bed she was sitting on.

"I try to avoid being at home," she said, "because every conversation turns into him telling me what I did wrong." Afraid to stand up to him, afraid to walk out of the room when he was raging, she tried to maintain her dignity and keep the peace. But she was losing self-respect, feeling more and more disempowered. And she was worried about how the constant fighting was affecting their teenage daughter. She didn't want to continue as things were, yet was unsure how to chart a path forward—unclear about her options.

Every choice has a price, something you gain, and something you lose. One choice we can always make is to do nothing. To decide not to decide. To keep on going the way we are. At the other extreme, Marina could decide to leave the relationship and file for divorce.

"You don't have to be stuck," I told her. "You don't have to sit there in a bad situation." However, I cautioned, a divorce can be an extreme way of continuing to do nothing. "What do you gain from a divorce? It gives you a piece of paper that says you're now free to marry someone else."

Divorce doesn't resolve the emotional business of the relationship. It just gives you legal permission to repeat the same pattern with someone else! It doesn't make you free. Whether Marina decided to leave her husband or stay in the marriage, her work was the same: to uncover the needs and expectations she brought to the marriage, and to heal the wounds she had brought with her, that she would keep carrying for the rest of her life until she dealt with them.

> EVERY CHOICE HAS A PRICE, SOMETHING YOU GAIN, AND SOMETHING YOU LOSE.

We examined her expectations first. "Did you know about your husband's anger when you married him?" I asked.

She shook her head vehemently. "He wins hearts," she said. An accomplished actor, he knows how to make his audience fall in love with him. Before they were married, she only saw this side of him—the charmer, the philosopher, the romantic. "Now the shoes fly."

"So what keeps you there?" I asked. As I've said, every behavior satisfies a need. Even an imprisoning and terrifying situation can serve us in some way. "Do you need the financial security? Or maybe you need the fighting?"

"I'm scared to be alone."

We all carry a fear of abandonment from infancy. But as she described her childhood in Western Europe, it was clear that her fear of abandonment had been compounded by outright neglect. When she was fourteen, her father said he could no longer stand to live with her mother, and left. He never once came back to visit his children—he didn't even call to check in. Marina's mother was too distraught to cope with the needs of the family, so Marina stepped in to fill the role, putting the younger children to bed, staying up late to bake bread and prepare food for the next day.

A year later, when the Berlin Wall came down, her mother made her own devastating announcement. She'd met an East German man through a newspaper ad. She was moving to former East Germany to be with him, taking the younger children with her. Marina would stay behind. She'd have to fend for herself. She handed Marina the rental agreement for a room in a house and left the next day. She didn't so much as call for more than a year.

The fact that Marina survived at all is a huge testament to her inner strength and resiliency. She stayed in the rental house for a few months until new tenants moved in, including a father who tried to seduce her, coming to her room at night with a glass of wine. She broke her lease, left school, and moved from town to town throughout Western Europe, working multiple jobs, house-sitting for people away on vacation, at one point living on an artists' commune, another time staying at a rehabilitation farm where people in recovery came to take care of horses. She developed a dangerous eating disorder, convinced that she must be a terrible person to have been left by both her parents, thinking that if she could make herself disappear, maybe her parents would finally notice she was missing. When Marina was sixteen, the owner of the rehab farm, herself an active alcoholic, turned Marina out. She stood on the street with a suitcase in each hand, homeless and alone. In despair, she called her mom and begged for help. But her mother was still steeped in her own struggle and refused.

"From that moment on, I knew I was completely alone in the world," Marina said.

In her early twenties, she moved to Berlin in search of better work opportunities, and through connections began to train with a performance group, living in an old trailer in the backyard of her school. It wasn't an easy life. The trailer was unheated. She froze her way through the fierce Berlin winters, endured rigorous training. But the new life suited her. While dancing, she felt strong and free. She couldn't starve herself and detach from her body anymore, and for the first time, she no longer wanted to. She had discovered passion and purpose: the joy of moving her body, the power of movement and expression.

She fell in love with another performer, who'd grown up in East Germany during the Cold War. It was difficult for him to communicate his emotions, to show love.

"Like my parents, I guess," Marina said ruefully.

Two years after they broke up, he died by suicide. Intellectually she knew his death wasn't her fault, that even if they'd stayed together, she couldn't have saved him. But the loss hit her hard.

"They found him a week or two after he died," she said. "He was completely alone."

We all go into relationships carrying messages we learned in childhood. Sometimes it's a literal phrase someone repeated—like when my mother told me, "A bad husband is better than no husband." Sometimes it's something we gleaned from others' actions or the home environment.

"Honey," I told Marina, "I'm hearing that you carry a message inside—that if you love someone, they'll leave you."

Tears sprang into her eyes. She wrapped her arms around herself as though the room had suddenly gone cold.

When we're imprisoned, it's the damaging messages that stick.

"But there's another message I hear in your story," I told her.

"That you're a woman of strength. Once you were that scared, lonely girl standing on the street with your suitcases. Many times you could have died, and you didn't. Now look at you. Out of something you didn't want, you made something good. *You're good*."

Believing at a fundamental level that she wasn't worthy of love, Marina had chosen a partner and patterns of behavior that reinforced this belief. I often see this dynamic in military marriages. When it's only a matter of time before you'll have to deploy or move and start your life anew, it's hard to trust that someone will really stick with you through the distance and disruption. One way to cope with the fear of how much it will hurt to be apart—or the fear that someone will leave us or be unfaithful—is to avoid being close. Marina had married a man who charmed her into feeling safe and adored, only to use their relationship as a punching bag. He was carrying his own pain into the relationship—and his method of coping with his unresolved emotional business, to rage and blame, just reinforced Marina's internalized message that to love is to be hurt and abandoned.

"Perhaps you're both using the fighting to fight intimacy," I said. "So let's look at your pattern."

Many couples have a three-step dance, a cycle of conflict they keep repeating. Step one is frustration. It's left to fester, and pretty soon they move on to step two: fighting. They yell or rage until they're tired, and fall into step three: making up. (Never have sex after a fight. It just reinforces the fighting!) Making up seems like the end of the conflict, but it's really a continuation of the cycle. The initial frustration hasn't been resolved. You've just set yourselves up for another go-round.

I wanted to give Marina some tools to help her stop the dance at step one. What were the frustration triggers that kept launching them into the same imprisoning dance?

"You're either contributing to the relationship or you're contaminating it," I said. "How do each of you contaminate the marriage?"

"When I want to have a discussion with him—express a feeling or bring something up—he's afraid of being guilty, that something's his fault." His preferred defense was offense—to turn the tables and attack Marina with blame and criticism.

"And what's your part in it?" I asked.

"I try to explain myself. Or I say, 'Stop,' and he explodes and starts kicking or throwing or smashing something."

I gave her an assignment, a detour to get them off the path they kept choosing. "The next time he tells you you're wrong, your answer is 'You're right.' He can't fight with that. And you're not lying, because everybody makes mistakes; anybody could improve. Just say, 'Yes, you're right.'"

If we deny an accusation, we're still accepting blame. We're taking responsibility for something that isn't ours.

"The next time he's angry, ask yourself, 'Whose problem is it?' Unless you caused the problem, you're not responsible when he tries to put the monkey on your back. Give the monkey back. Say, 'Sounds like you're in a tough position. Sounds like you're mad about that.' When he tries to make his feelings about you, give the feeling back to him.

**IF WE DENY AN ACCUSATION, WE'RE STILL ACCEPTING BLAME.**

It's his feeling to face and you hope he'll let go. When you step into the ring, he's looking at you, not at his feeling. Stop rescuing him."

When Marina and I spoke a few weeks later, she said the de-escalation tools were working. Their fights had radically diminished.

"But I have so much resentment against him," she said. This time, it wasn't his anger she wanted to talk about. It was her own. "In my mind, I make him responsible for everything."

"So do the opposite," I said. "Thank him."

She stared at me, eyebrows raised in surprise.

"You choose your attitude. So thank him. And thank your parents, too. They're helping you become a very good survivor."

"And just ignore what happened? Leave out what they did?"

"Make peace with it."

Many of us didn't have the loving and caring parents we desired and deserved. Maybe they were preoccupied, angry, worried, depressed. Maybe we were born at the wrong time, in a season of friction or loss or financial strain. Maybe our caregivers were dealing with their own trauma, and they weren't always responsive to our needs for attention and affection. Maybe they didn't pick us up and say, "We always wanted a child just like you."

"You're grieving over the parents you never had," I told Marina. "And you can grieve over the husband you don't have."

Grief helps us face and ultimately release what happened or didn't happen. And it opens up space to see what *is* and choose where we go from here.

"Would you like to be married to you?" I asked.

She gave me a confused look.

"What do you like about you?"

She was silent, her brow creased as though taken aback, or maybe she was just searching for the words.

She began hesitantly, but her voice became fuller as she spoke. Her eyes brightened and a flush rose in her cheeks.

"I like that I care about other people," she said. "I like that I have passion—that I love climbing high. I like that I don't give up."

"Write it down, honey," I said. "Carry those words in your purse."

Taking an honest inventory is so important. It's easy to reach for critiques of others and ourselves, to focus on wrongs and complaints. But all of us are good. We choose what we focus on.

"What's good about your husband?" I asked.

She paused, squinting slightly, as though trying to see into the distance. "He cares," she said. "Even though he is like he is, I know he cares about me. And he's working hard. I injured my shoulder, and he helped me. There are times when he supports me."

"Are you stronger with him, or without him?"

Only you can decide if a relationship depletes or empowers you. But it's not a question to answer quickly. You can't know the truth about your relationships until you deal with your own wounds, until you bury and leave behind all the things from the past you're still dragging around.

My decision to divorce Béla was unkind and unnecessary, but it was useful in one way: it created more silence and space for me to start to face my past and my grief. It didn't liberate me from my emotions and trauma, from flashbacks, from feeling numb, anxious, isolated, and afraid. Only I could do that.

"Be careful what you do when you're restless," my sister Magda had warned me. "You can start to think the wrong things. He's too this, he's too that, I've suffered enough. You end up missing the same things that drove you crazy."

And I did miss Béla. The way he danced and wore joy on his sleeve. His relentless humor, how he made me laugh in spite of myself. His steadfast appetite for risk.

Two years after our divorce, we remarried. But we didn't return to the same marriage we'd had before. We weren't resigned to each other; we'd chosen each other anew, and this time without the distorted lens of resentment and unmet expectations.

"Your husband is getting your anger," I told Marina. "But maybe he's not the one you're really angry with."

We cast others in the roles that help us enact the story we've decided to tell. When we tell a new story—when we come home to our wholeness—our relationships might improve. Or we might find that we don't need them anymore, that they don't have a place in the story of freedom.

You don't have to figure it out in a hurry. In fact, it's best to stop figuring and figuring and trying to understand. It's an answer that will come only by playing more, by living your life as fully as possible, and being who you already are: a person of strength.

# KEYS TO FREE YOURSELF
# FROM RESENTMENT

- *Change the dance steps. Many couples have a three-step dance, a cycle of conflict they keep repeating. It starts with frustration, escalates to fighting, and appears to restore harmony when they make up. Until the initial frustration is resolved, the peace won't last for long. What frustration triggers keep going unresolved in your relationship? How can you change the dance at step one, before you fall into the old cycle? Decide on one thing to do differently the next time frustration brews. Then do it. Take note of how it went and celebrate any change.*

- *Take care of your own emotional business. Reflect on a message about love that you may have learned as a child and may be carrying into your relationships. For example, Marina was carrying the message that if you love someone, they leave. What did your childhood teach you about love? Fill in this sentence:* If you love someone, _____.

- *Would you like to be married to you? What qualities do you think create a comfortable and thriving relationship? Would you like to be married to someone such as you? What strengths do you bring to the table? Make a list. What behaviors might be challenging to live with? Make a list. Are you living in a way that brings out your best self?*

# CHAPTER 9

# Are You Evolving or Revolving?

## The Prison of Paralyzing Fear

I'd been teaching psychology at a high school in El Paso for a few years—and had even been awarded teacher of the year—when I decided to return to school for a master's in educational psychology. One day my clinical supervisor came to me and said, "Edie, you've got to get a doctorate."

I laughed. "By the time I get a doctorate I'll be fifty," I said.

"You'll be fifty anyway."

Those are the smartest four words anyone ever said to me.

Honey, you're going to be fifty anyway—or thirty or sixty or ninety. So you might as well take a risk. Do something you've never done before. Change is synonymous with growth. To grow, you've got to evolve instead of revolve.

In America, the slang term for a psychologist is *shrink*. But I like to call myself a stretch! To meet survivor to survivor, and guide you to release your self-limiting beliefs and embrace your potential.

I studied Latin as a girl, and I love the phrase *Tempura mutantur, et nos mutamur in illis*. Times are changing, and we are changing with the times. We aren't stuck in the past, or stuck in our old patterns and behaviors. We're here now, in the present, and it's up to us what we hold on to, what we let go, and what we reach for.

Gloria is still carrying a heavy burden. She fled the civil war in El Salvador when she was four, grew up in an extremely violent household where her mother was repeatedly beaten by her father, and then, when she was thirteen and visiting family in El Salvador, was raped by her pastor uncle, the man who had christened her. He assaulted her on Christmas Eve, destroying her faith along with her sense of safety. No one believed her when she came forward about the assault, and the uncle who raped her is still a practicing pastor.

"I'm holding on to so much anguish and hurt," she said. "Everything is covered in fear. I don't want to lose my husband or children to the past. I need things to change, but I just don't know how to change, or where to start."

She thought that pursuing a degree in social work might help her find purpose in the present and unlock the hold of the past, but hearing her clients' experiences of victimization only deepened her sense of despair and helplessness, and she abandoned the degree. She hated feeling defeated, hated that her children saw her struggling. Now, along with the frequent intrusions and feeling of panic from the past, she lives every day terrified that her children will be harmed the way she was.

"I do my best to make sure they're safe," she said. "But I won't always be there to protect them. I don't want them to live in fear. I don't want to pass on the fear."

But everyday events, like dropping her daughter off at camp, provoke enormous fear. "I'm up all night, thinking, 'What's going to happen to her? Is something happening to her right now?'"

We should never stop seeking safety and justice, doing everything in our power to protect ourselves, our loved ones, our neighbors, our fellow humans. But we have a choice how much of our lives we give over to fear.

Fear uses the most insistent, relentless, provocative words: *what if, what if, what if?* When fear comes like a panic storm, and your body shakes and your heart races and the trauma you already survived threatens to swallow you, take your own precious hand and say, "Thank you, fear, for wanting to protect me." Then say, "That was then, this is now." Say it over and over again. You already made it. Here you are. Wrap your arms around yourself and rub your own shoulders. "Attagirl," you say. "Love you."

You never know what's coming from the outside. You can't predict who might show up to cause harm—yell an insult, throw a punch, break a promise, betray your trust, drop a bomb, start a war. I wish I could tell you that tomorrow the world will be safe from cruelty and violence and prejudice, from rape and depravity and genocide. But that world may not ever come. We live in a world with danger, and so we live in a world with fear. Your safety *isn't* guaranteed.

**FEAR AND LOVE DON'T COEXIST.**

But fear and love don't coexist. And fear doesn't have to rule your life.

Releasing the fear starts with you.

* * *

When we've been hurt or betrayed, it isn't easy to let go of the fear that we'll be hurt again.

Fear's favorite words are "I told you so." *I told you* you'd regret it. *I told you* it was too risky. *I told you* it wouldn't turn out well.

And we hate to disappoint our hunches.

We hold on to fear, thinking vigilance will protect us, but fear becomes a relentless cycle, a self-fulfilling prophecy. A better protection against suffering is to know how to love and forgive yourself, to be safe for yourself, to not punish yourself for the mistakes and hurt and pain that are inevitable parts of life.

This was Kathleen's struggle when I spoke with her in the aftermath of her husband's affair.

She'd been happily enjoying her twelfth year of marriage to a handsome, accomplished doctor, taking a pause in her career to focus on their young sons, when she got the phone call. A man she'd never heard of claimed to run an escort service and threatened to expose her husband's affair with one of the escorts and ruin his career if she didn't pay up. It was sordid and outlandish, the stuff of soap operas and nightmares. But when she confronted her husband, he said it was true. He'd engaged the services of an escort. The man who'd called Kathleen was her pimp.

Kathleen went into a state of shock. She shook uncontrollably, she couldn't eat or sleep. Her world was upside down and inside out. How had she been so oblivious to the truth? She entered a state of perpetual vigilance, prodding her life for clues that would help her understand why her husband had cheated, and for evidence that he might be straying again.

But over time—and with lots of help from a marriage counselor—the infidelity became an opportunity for her and her husband to rediscover their marriage, to rekindle intimacy. As they regained stability, he surprised her by becoming more attentive and romantic. Their marriage felt more joyful. They hosted a giant Christmas party, their house full of light. On Valentine's Day, her husband woke her before dawn and led her down the dark hall to the staircase bedecked in rose petals and twinkling tea lights. They sat in their robes together and cried. Sweetness and trust had returned to their relationship.

Little did she know he was weeks away from another destructive decision—the start of another affair with a young colleague—or that in a few months she would stumble on a passionate letter that he'd written to his lover.

Kathleen and I spoke two years after the devastating discovery that he'd betrayed her again. She chose to stay in the marriage, and once more they engaged in intensive couples therapy and rebuilt their relationship, from the ground up. She told me that in many ways their bond feels stronger than ever. Her husband is less walled off, less prone to edginess, more affectionate—he hugs and kisses and comforts her, checks in frequently, video calls her from work or dials out from his work phone so she knows he's really where he says he is. He's open about why he cheated again—"I was a powerful narcissist, trying to have it all," he says—and speaks his heartfelt regret.

But Kathleen is still imprisoned by fear.

"I have the loving, attentive husband I've always wanted," she said. "But I can't accept it. I can't believe it. I play the mind movies all day, reliving the past, waiting for the other shoe to drop, for him to cheat again. I know that I'm robbing myself of my own life. I know I need to learn to trust him again. I'm trying to stay in the present. But I can't escape the fear. I can't stop policing and monitoring him."

When we're living with a lot of doubt, we're on the lookout for signs that will calm—or confirm!—our fears. But whatever we're looking for on the outside, we need to address within.

"Maybe it's not your husband that you're doubting," I said. "Maybe it's you. I heard you say four times, 'I can't.' "

Her bright eyes filled with tears.

"You're not giving yourself enough credit. So let's work on dissolving that self-doubt."

The prison of fear can become a catalyst for growth and empowerment. To enact this transformation, language is one of our most powerful tools.

"Let's start with that 'I can't,' " I told her. "First of all, it's a lie. *I can't* means I'm helpless. And unless you're an infant, that simply isn't true."

When we say "I can't," what we're really saying is "I won't." *I won't accept it. I won't believe. I won't escape the fear. I won't stop policing and monitoring him.* The language of fear is the language of resistance. And if we're resisting, we're working very hard to ensure that we go nowhere. We deny growth and curiosity. We're revolving, not evolving, shutting down opportunities for change.

I asked Kathleen to eliminate *I can't* from her vocabulary.

If you're going to take away something, you'll be more successful if you can replace it with something else. If you're skipping a cocktail, replace it with another beverage you enjoy. If you want to stop withdrawing and hiding from a loved one, like Robin in an earlier chapter, replace the habit of leaving the room with staying, with regarding your partner with a smile and kind eyes.

I told Kathleen, "Anytime you start to say 'I can't,' replace it with 'I can.'" I *can* let go of the past. I *can* stay in the present. I *can* love and trust myself.

I pointed her to two more fear-based phrases she'd used back-to-back in the first minute of our conversation: *I'm trying* and *I need to*.

"You said you're trying to live in the present," I said. "But trying is lying. You're either doing it or you're not." If you say, "I'm trying," you don't actually have to do it. You let yourself off the hook. "It's time to stop trying and start doing."

When we're on the cusp of taking action, many of us use the phrase "I need to." It sounds like we're identifying goals and setting priorities. Kathleen wanted to change the relentless fear and vigilance in her marriage, and she said, "I know *I need to* learn to trust him again."

"But that's another lie," I told her. "Needs are things without which we can't survive. Breathing, sleeping, eating."

We can stop burdening and pressuring ourselves, telling ourselves that something is necessary for our survival when it isn't. And we can stop looking at our choices as obligations.

"You don't *need* to trust your husband," I said. "You *want* to. And if you want to, you can choose to."

When we talk as though we're forced or obligated or incapable, that's how we're going to think, which means that's also how we'll feel, and consequently, how we'll behave. We become captives to fear: I need to do this, *or else*; I want to do that, *but I can't*. To free yourself from the prison, pay attention to your language. Lis-

> **LISTEN FOR THE *I CAN'T*, THE *I'M TRYING*, THE *I NEED TO*, AND THEN SEE IF YOU CAN REPLACE THESE IMPRISONING PHRASES WITH SOMETHING ELSE: *I CAN, I WANT, I'M WILLING, I CHOOSE*.**

ten for the *I can't*, the *I'm trying*, the *I need to*, and then see if you can replace these imprisoning phrases with something else: *I can, I want, I'm willing, I choose.* This is the language that empowers us to change.

Kathleen doesn't have any guarantees that her husband won't cheat again. If she leaves the marriage, she has no foolproof armor against being betrayed by someone else. But she has tools to free herself from paralysis.

Whose responsibility is it if your dreams and behaviors aren't aligned? One patient said he felt he would be more on top of things at work and more patient with his family if he had better sleep habits—but he was still drinking five cups of coffee. Another patient longed for a stable, committed relationship, but she kept waking up in a different man's bed. These patients' goals and choices didn't match. I'm all for positive thinking, but it goes nowhere unless it's followed by positive action.

And we can stop working so hard to go nowhere.

One of the ways we resist change is by being hard on ourselves. A patient told me she wanted to lose weight, but when she came to see me she'd spend half the session berating herself. "I'm pigging out on ice cream," she'd say. "I'm pigging out on chocolate cake." The minute you put yourself down, you're never going to change. But if you say, "Today I'm not going to put sugar in my cappuccino," then you're *doing* something about it. This is how growth and learning and healing happen—by what you do, little by little, on your own behalf.

Sometimes seemingly trivial changes can have a big impact.

Michelle, who had struggled for years with anorexia, had always avoided doughnuts. She'd been afraid of them her whole life—afraid that if she ate one, she'd eat the whole box. Afraid that if she let herself indulge in even one small bite, she'd become fat in an instant. Afraid that she would lose control. Afraid that if she gave herself permission to experience pleasure, if she dared to let go, she'd fall apart.

But she knew that as long as she lived in fear of an old-fashioned glazed, she was still in prison. One morning she summoned her courage, walked into a bakery—even the jingly bell on the door and the smell of sugar made her sweat—and bought two doughnuts and brought them to her therapy session. In a supportive place, with the comfort of her therapist sharing the experience, Michelle let herself feel the fear, all those deep-seated anxieties about her self-image and self-worth, about losing control. And then she got curious about the experience. Together, she and her therapist took bites of doughnut. Michelle felt the crunch of the glazed icing on her tongue. The soft, cakey texture when she bit in. The rush of sugar flooding her body. She turned her anxiety into excitement!

We aren't born with fear. Somewhere along the way, we learn it.

I'll never forget the day when Audrey was ten. She had a friend over and they were playing in her room. Just as I walked past her open door with a basket of laundry, an ambulance screamed by, siren blaring, a sound that even now continues to startle me. I was amazed to see Audrey dive straight under her bed. Her friend stared at her, baffled by her reaction. Somehow, probably by seeing *me* jump at the sound of a siren, my daughter had learned to be afraid. She'd internalized my fear.

Often the emotional responses that get ingrained in us aren't even our own—they're ones we've learned from watching others. So you can ask yourself, "Is this my fear? Or someone else's?" If the fear really belongs to your mother or father or grandparent or spouse, you don't have to carry it anymore. Just put it down. Release your hold. Leave it behind.

> WE AREN'T BORN WITH FEAR. SOMEWHERE ALONG THE WAY, WE LEARN IT.

Then make a list of the fears that remain.

This is how you begin to face your fears, rather than fighting them, or running from them, or medicating them.

I did this fear exercise with my patient Alison, the professional singer. She was struggling in the wake of a divorce, and dealing with some physical ailments—a vocal tremor, back pain—that hindered her ability to perform. Her list of fears included:

*Being alone.*
*Losing my income.*
*Being poor, possibly homeless.*
*Being sick and not having anyone there to help me.*
*Not being accepted by others.*

I asked her to go over her list and decide how realistic each fear was. If it was realistic—a valid concern given the facts of her life— she circled it and put an R next to it. If the fear was unrealistic, she crossed it off her list. She discovered that two of her fears weren't realistic. With income from royalties and retirement savings, she had a safety net. Even if she lost income, which was likely given the tours she'd had to cancel, it wasn't likely that she'd lose her house and end up on the streets. She crossed off *being poor, possibly homeless*. She also crossed off *not being accepted by others*. Events in her life showed a different truth—that she was an admired performer, a cherished friend. More important, she realized that whether or not she was accepted by someone else wasn't up to her. She was learning to love herself. What others thought about her was up to them.

The three remaining fears got Rs: *being alone, losing my income,* and *being sick and not having anyone there to help me.*

I asked her to generate a list of things she could do today on her own behalf to protect herself and build the life she wanted. If she was afraid of being alone and wanted to be in a relationship again, she could sign up on a dating app, spend a day making eye contact with strangers (you never know who you'll meet!), go to a Codependents Anonymous meeting so she could enter a new relationship in a healthier place than she'd been when she married her ex. To face her fear of being sick with no one to take care of her, she could research resources available should she be in need of care. What home health organizations were in the area? What did they cost? Were they covered by insurance? And so on. It's not that we make our fears go away. We don't let them dominate. We invite the other voices in the room to do some talking. And then we *do* something. We take charge. We ask for help.

Often when we're stuck it's not that we don't know *what* to do. It's that we're afraid we won't do it well enough. We're self-critical. We hold high standards. We want others' approval—most of all, our own—and think we can earn it by being Superman or Superwoman. But if you're perfectionistic, you're going to procrastinate, because perfect means never.

Here's another way to think about it. If you're perfectionistic, you're competing with God. And you're human. You're going to make mistakes. Don't try to beat God, because God will always win.

It doesn't take courage to strive for perfection. It takes courage to be average. To say, "I'm okay with me." To say, "Good enough is good enough."

Sometimes our fears are painfully realistic, our resources for meeting them limited.

This was the case for Lauren, the mother of two young children who, in her early forties, was diagnosed with cancer. Her disease was its own prison. Her fears about the future—about dying, about her children growing up without her—became a second set of bars. One day she told me what scared her most of all—that she would die without having really lived. She was trapped in an emotionally and physically abusive marriage. She longed to protect her children and live free from her husband's control and violence. But it seemed impossible to leave. Cancer had rendered her physically and financially vulnerable, compounding an already dangerous situation. To leave seemed too big a risk.

We explored the fact that there's a difference between stress and distress. Distress is constant threat and uncertainty, like we had in Auschwitz—when we took a shower, we never knew what was going to come out of the spigot, water or gas. Distress is toxic. It can mean never knowing when a bomb will drop on your house, never knowing where you will sleep each night. Stress, on the other hand, is actually a good thing. It requires us to face a challenge, to find creative solutions, to trust ourselves.

> THERE'S A DIFFERENCE BETWEEN STRESS AND DISTRESS. DISTRESS IS CONSTANT THREAT AND UNCERTAINTY. STRESS, ON THE OTHER HAND, IS ACTUALLY A GOOD THING.

It is so challenging and dangerous to leave the cycle of abuse that most women return multiple times to their abuser before breaking free—if they ever do. It would no doubt be challenging for Lauren, too. She would likely struggle—to feed her children on a limited income, to manage a household and her treatment regimen as a single parent. But she would no longer be living every day under the threat of violence. She would no longer be in distress.

Yet leaving would require her to exchange a known reality for an unknown one. This is usually what stops us from taking risks. We'd rather stick with what we know, painful or untenable as it is, than face what we don't know.

When you risk, you *don't* know how it will turn out. It's possible that you won't get what you want, that things will be worse. But you'll still be better off, because you'll be living in the world as it is, not in an imaginary reality created by your fear.

Lauren decided to leave her husband. She said, "I don't know how much time I have left. I'm not going to spend the rest of my life being told I'm worthless."

When I witness patients going nowhere, spinning on a relentless merry-go-round of self-destructive behavior, I confront them.

"Why are you choosing a self-destructive life? Do you want to die?"

They say, "Yes, sometimes I do."

It's a profoundly human question: *To be or not to be?*

I hope you always choose to be. You're going to be dead anyway someday, and you'll be dead for a very long time. Why not become curious? Why not see what this life has to offer you?

Curiosity is vital. It's what allows us to risk. When we're full of fear, we're living in a past that already happened, or a future that hasn't arrived. When we're curious, we're here in the present, eager to discover what's going to happen next. It's better to risk and grow, and maybe fail, than to remain imprisoned, never knowing what could have been.

# KEYS TO FREE YOURSELF FROM PARALYZING FEAR

- *I can. I want. I'm willing.* For one day, keep track of every time you say I can't, I need, I should, and I'm trying. "I can't" means I won't. "I need" and "I should" mean I'm abdicating my freedom of choice. And "I'm trying" is lying. Eliminate this language from your vocabulary. You can't let go of something unless you replace it with something else. Replace the language of fear with something else: I can, I want, I'm willing, I choose, I am.

- *Change is synonymous with growth.* Do one thing differently today than you did yesterday. If you always drive the same way to work, take a different route—or ride your bike or take a bus. If you're usually too rushed or preoccupied to chat with the checker at the grocery store, try making eye contact and conversation. If your family is usually too busy to eat together, try sitting down to a meal together without the TV on or cell phones at the table. These small steps might seem inconsequential, but they actually train your brain to know that you're capable of change, that nothing is locked in stone, that your choices and possibilities are endless. And getting curious about your life helps turn your anxiety into excitement. You don't have to stay where you are, how you are, doing what you're doing. Mix things up. You're not stuck.

- *Identify your fears.* Make a list of your fears. For each fear, ask, "Is this my fear? Or someone else's?" If it's a fear you've inherited or taken on, cross it off your list. Let it go. It isn't yours to carry. For each remaining fear, decide how realistic it is. If it is a valid concern given the facts of your life, circle it. For each realistic fear, decide if it causes you distress or stress. Distress is chronic danger and uncertainty. If you're living in distress, your foremost responsibility is to tend to your safety and survival needs, to the degree that this is possible. Do whatever is in your power to protect yourself. If the fear is causing you stress, acknowledge that stress can be healthy. Notice how stress might be giving you an opportunity to grow. Finally, for each of the realistic fears, generate a list of things you could do today on your own behalf to strengthen yourself and build the life you want.

# CHAPTER 10

# The Nazi in You

## The Prison of Judgment

When Audrey and I were in Lausanne, Switzerland, last year, I gave a keynote address to an inspiring group of global executives and leadership coaches at the International Institute of Management Development, one of Europe's top business schools. At the dinner after my address the guests stunned me with their heartfelt toasts of thanks and appreciation. One man in particular struck me. He was tall, with wavy hair beginning to gray, his thin face dominated by sad, intellectual eyes. He said that my words about forgiveness, in particular, had felt like a gift. Then he began to cry. Tears streaming down his face, he said, "I have a story, too. It is so hard to tell it."

Audrey caught my eye. Something passed between us, a silent recognition of trauma's collateral damage, the pain that's passed on when a secret is kept. When the formal meal concluded, she excused herself and threaded her way through the crowded room to the man's table. When she returned, she said, "His name is Andreas and you definitely need to hear his story."

Our schedule was packed, but Audrey arranged for me to have a private lunch with Andreas the next day, before we flew home. In a quiet, thoughtful way, he laid out the pieces of his personal history, jigsaw moments of realization that he had put together over time.

In the first puzzle piece, he's nine years old and stands with his father at an exhibition in a small village outside Frankfurt. "Son, this is a list of all the mayors of this town," his father intones, pointing with a heavy finger to one name: Hermann Neumann. Hermann is Andreas's middle name. His father's finger taps the name, his tone a peculiar mix of sorrow, anger, longing, and pride as he says, "This is your grandfather."

Andreas's grandfather died a decade before he was born. He had no personal frame of reference, no idea what sort of man he'd been, what it felt like to sit on his knee or hear him tell a story. No one spoke of his grandfather. Instead there was a weighty silence in the place where the family patriarch should have been. Andreas sensed that his absent grandfather had something to do with the darkness that sometimes crept into his father's and uncles' eyes. He was too young to understand that there was only one way that someone would have been given a formal administrative post in Germany during the years 1933 to 1945.

It was another nine years before the next puzzle piece crystallized. Andreas had just returned to Germany after a year as an exchange student in Chile. His uncle, after years of struggling with alcoholism, had just passed away, and Andreas went to his apartment to clear out the basement storage space. He stood in the dim room, letting his eyes adjust, surveying the shelves packed with books and belongings, trying to predict how long it would take to empty them, when he saw it. An old wooden suitcase pasted with a sticker that was oddly familiar. He stepped closer, and realized it was a customs sticker from Arica, Chile, stamped with the year 1931. The leather tag on the suitcase bore his grandfather's name. Why had no one in the family mentioned, when he left for Chile, that his grandfather had also traveled there? And why did finding the suitcase make him feel so unsettled?

He asked his parents about it. His father shrugged and left the room. His mother spoke in vague terms. "I think he was involved in something or other," she said, "and left for a few months." The early thirties had been a time of dire economic crisis in Germany. Maybe his grandfather had sought opportunity elsewhere, as other young Germans did during those lean years. Andreas convinced himself this was true, and did his best to ignore the nagging feeling that there was more to the story.

A few years later, he asked his father's other brother for permission to go through old family documents and memorabilia stored in the back of his house. Instinct told him that he might find in his grandfather's past something that could explain the trench of unrest that linked the generations of his family—his father's and uncles' struggles with alcohol, their shrouded, closed-off manner that Andreas sensed had something to do with shame.

He read and sorted for days, and little by little, more pieces emerged. His grandfather's old passport, stamped by immigration in Chile, showing his arrival in 1930 and departure in 1931. A telegram sent to his grandfather in 1942 at his job in Frankfurt where he worked as an office clerk for one of the big industrial conglomerates. *Have you removed all the bicycles and belongings from the house in Frankfurt?* the telegram read, signed by his grandfather's brother. A peculiar message.

Then Andreas read the return address. His great-uncle had sent the message to his grandfather from the Gestapo headquarters in Marseille. How had his great-uncle been allowed to access a Nazi Telex machine? Why had his grandfather received a personal message from a Gestapo office? How deep did his family's Nazi connection go?

He kept digging through documents and found a letter from a family friend, notifying them that his great-uncle had died during the war on a withdrawal mission in France when his car went over a mine. No personal effects or ID tags had been recovered from the explosion. He also discovered letters from his grandfather to his grandmother, written from a prisoner-of-war camp in southern Germany after the war. What alleged or actual offenses had put his grandfather in prison?

He searched for years for more information, but hit only dead ends. Despite his grandfather's imprisonment, there didn't appear to be any evidence of a trial or an investigation into his grandfather's criminal acts. In a last-ditch effort to fill in the blanks in his family's past, Andreas contacted archives of the home state where his grandparents had lived after the war. At last, he was handed a slim file. There were only a few sheets of paper inside, including a typed chronology that filled just half the page.

In 1927, when he was twenty years old, his grandfather had joined the SA—the Sturmabteilung, the first Nazi Party paramilitary group established to persecute Jews by throwing stones through windows and setting fire to city blocks, creating a climate of fear and violence and contributing to Hitler's rise to power. He left the SA in 1930—the year he'd gone to Chile—only to return to Germany a few months later, rejoin the SA, and rise in the ranks to become a squad leader and a member of the Nazi

Party. These decisions in 1933 facilitated his job at the finance administration office in Frankfurt, and his mayorship in the village where Andreas's father had pointed to his name—Hermann Neumann—the four syllables that denoted the dark legacy he'd inherited.

"I share his name," Andreas said. "My cells stem from his cells. In a foundational way, I'm a result—a product—of what happened."

His very identity felt contaminated.

And history seemed to be repeating. At the same time that he learned the truth about his grandfather, the right-wing movement was gaining energy in an economically devastated eastern Germany.

"I saw pictures of people running after immigrants in Chemnitz," he said, "and I knew my grandfather had done the same."

He officially changed his middle name from Hermann to Phileas, after the character Phileas Fogg in Jules Verne's *Around the World in Eighty Days*, a book that sparked Andreas's curiosity about the world during his childhood days. The name change was an act to distance himself from his grandfather, to sever the personal connection to his grandfather's wrongs, to say, "Yes, I am Hermann's grandson, and I don't need to carry his first name."

Andreas said he is still trying to release the burden of the past—the relentless shame that he carries the blood of a perpetrator, that his very life came into being as a result of the benefits his grandfather garnered from hurting others, from injustice. It's a collective guilt that many German people unfortunately carry. If you are German, or Hutu, or a descendant of those who enforced apartheid or genocide or another instance of systemic violence and injustice, I am telling you: it wasn't you. Assign the blame to the perpetrators, and then decide.

"How long are you going to keep picking this up and carrying it around?" I asked Andreas. "What's the legacy *you* want to pass on?"

Do you want to stay beholden to the past? Or can you find a way to release your loved ones—and yourself?

Until our trip to Europe, I had no idea how much my own daughter was struggling with this question.

Neither Audrey nor I remember ever speaking of my past during her childhood. She learned about the Holocaust at Sunday school and asked Béla about it. He told her I'd been in Auschwitz. Something clicked into place. She'd sensed the presence of things we weren't talking about; she knew there was pain. Yet because she didn't know to ask—or at some level didn't want to know— the truth had remained hidden.

Now it was in full view. When I began to talk more openly and publicly about my past, Audrey didn't know what to do with the feelings my history elicited in her. She wondered how my suffering, and Béla's, too, might have transferred to her DNA, and worried she would pass the burden of trauma on to her own children. For years, she avoided books, films, museums, and events that dealt with the Holocaust.

When we carry a difficult legacy, we often react in one of two ways: we resist it or detach from it; we fight it or run away. Though from opposite sides of the same tragedy, Andreas and Audrey were walking the same path: reckoning with a brutal truth, and figuring out how to hold it and carry it forward.

\*     \*     \*

Other than staying silent in an effort to protect my children from my pain, I hadn't considered the broader impact of legacy until the early 1980s, when a fourteen-year-old boy came to his court-appointed therapy session wearing a brown shirt and brown boots, leaned his elbow on the table, and started ranting about how to make America white again,

> TO STOP BIGOTRY MEANS YOU START WITH YOURSELF. YOU LET GO OF JUDGMENT AND CHOOSE COMPASSION.

about how to kill all the Jews, niggers, Mexicans, and chinks. Fury swept through me. I wanted so badly to shake him, to say, "How dare you talk like that? Do you know who I am? My mother died in a gas chamber!" Just when I thought I might reach out my hands and throttle him, I heard a voice within say, "Find the bigot in you."

Impossible, I thought. I'm not a bigot. I'm a Holocaust survivor and an immigrant. I lost my parents to hate. I used the "colored" bathroom at the factory in Baltimore in solidarity with my African American coworkers. I marched for civil rights with Dr. Martin Luther King Jr. I'm not a bigot!

But to stop bigotry means you start with yourself. You let go of judgment and choose compassion.

I took a deep breath, leaned in, gazed at him with as much kindness as I could muster, and said, "Tell me more."

It was a tiny gesture of acceptance—not of his ideology, but of his personhood. And it was enough for him to speak a little of his lonely childhood, absentee parents, and severe neglect. Hearing his story reminded me that he hadn't joined an extremist group because he was born with hate. He was seeking what we all want:

acceptance, attention, affection. It's not an excuse. But attacking him would only nourish the seeds of worthlessness his upbringing had sown. I had the choice to alienate him further, or give him another version of refuge and belonging.

I never saw him again. I don't know if he continued on the path of prejudice, crime, and violence, or if he was able to heal and turn his life around. I do know that he walked in ready to kill someone like me, and he left in a softer mood.

Even a Nazi can be a messenger of God. This boy was my teacher, guiding me to the choice I always have to replace judgment with compassion—to recognize our shared humanity and practice love.

All over the world, a resurgence of fascism looms. My great-grandsons stand to inherit a world still gripped by prejudice and hate, where children yell racial epithets on the playground and carry guns to school, where nations build walls to deny asylum to fellow humans. In this state of fear and vulnerability, it's tempting to hate the haters. But I feel sorry for people who are taught to hate.

And I identify with them. What if I'd been born a German gentile instead of a Hungarian Jew? What if I'd heard Hitler proclaim, "Today, Germany, tomorrow, the world"? I, too, could have been a Hitler Youth, a guard at Ravensbrück.

We're not all descendants of Nazis. But we each have a Nazi within.

Freedom means choosing, every moment, whether we reach for our inner Nazi or our inner Gandhi. For the love we were born with or the hate we learned.

The inner Nazi is the part of you that has the capacity to judge and withhold compassion, that denies you the permission to be free and victimizes others when things don't go your way.

I'm still learning to let go of my inner Nazi.

I had lunch the other day at a fancy country club with women looking like a million dollars, every one of them. *Why am I spending an afternoon with people who look like Barbie dolls?* I thought. Then I caught myself in the act of judging others, engaging in the same us-versus-them mentality that killed my parents. When I put my prejudice aside, I discovered that the women were deep thinkers, that they'd experienced difficulty and pain. I'd been ready to write them off out of hand.

Another evening I spoke at a Chabad where a fellow survivor was in attendance. During the question-and-answer period following my talk, he asked, "Why did you fall into line so easily in Auschwitz? Why didn't you rebel?" His voice rose as he spoke. I started to explain that if I'd tried to fight a guard, I would have been shot right away. Rebellion wouldn't have freed me. I'd have missed out on the rest of my life. But then I realized I was reacting to his agitation by trying to defend my choices in the past. What about the present moment? Perhaps this was the one opportunity I'd have in my life to offer this man compassion. "Thank you so much for being here," I said. "Thank you for sharing your experience."

When we live in the prison of judgment, we don't just victimize others. We victimize ourselves.

Alex was on a journey toward self-compassion when we met. She showed me the tattoo on her arm. RAGE, it said. And then below, LOVE.

"That's how I grew up," she said. "My dad was rage. My mom was love."

Her father was a police officer who raised her and her brother in a climate of *wipe that look off your face; don't be a burden; show no emotion; act like you're fine; mistakes aren't allowed.* He often came home charged up about work, and Alex learned early to retreat to her room when his anger started to boil.

"I always thought it was my fault," she told me. "I didn't know what he was so upset about. No one ever told me, 'This isn't about you. You didn't do anything wrong.' I grew up thinking *I* was the one who made him angry, that there was something wrong with me."

This sense of blame and judgment became so internalized that as an adult she was afraid to ask a store clerk to retrieve an item from a high shelf.

"I was sure they'd think, 'What an idiot.'"

Alcohol provided temporary relief from her inhibitions, worry, and fear. Until she ended up in rehab.

When I spoke to Alex, she'd been sober for thirteen years and had recently left the strenuous emergency dispatcher job she'd worked at for more than twenty years, which was difficult to balance with the needs of her disabled daughter. This is a new theme in her life: to respond to herself with kindness.

And it's a goal she feels is thwarted every time she is with her family. While her mom embodies warmth, safety, kindness, and love, serving as the family peacekeeper, able to go with the flow, dropping everything to be there for her kids and grandkids, making even a routine family dinner feel as special as a holiday, Alex's dad is still angry and brooding. She monitors him with a watchful eye, reading his behavior so she can protect herself.

On a recent camping trip with her parents, she noticed all the negative comments her dad made about other people.

"The people next door were packing up their campsite and my dad said, 'This is my favorite part—when I watch the idiots try to figure out what they're doing.' That's how I grew up. My father watching and laughing when people make mistakes. No wonder I used to assume people were thinking terrible things about me! No wonder I used to watch him for any sign of a twitch or grimace—a clue to do whatever I could to keep him from getting angry. He scared me my whole life."

"The most obnoxious person is your best teacher," I told her. "He teaches you what you don't like in him, to examine in yourself. So how much time do you spend judging yourself? Scaring yourself?"

We looked at the ways she shut *herself* down. The Spanish class she wanted to take but didn't dare sign up for, the gym she was afraid to join.

We're all victims of victims. How far back do you want to go, searching for the source? It's better to start with yourself.

A few months later, Alex shared that she'd worked up the courage and self-acceptance to register for the Spanish class and join the gym. "I've been welcomed with open arms," she said. "They've even recruited me to compete with the women's power-lifting team."

When we relinquish our inner Nazi, we disarm the internal and external forces that have been holding us back.

"Half of you is your father," I told Alex. "Throw white light his way. Wrap him up in white light."

It's what I learned in Auschwitz. If I tried to fight the guards, I'd be shot. If I tried to flee, I'd run into the barbed wire and be electrocuted. So I turned my hatred into pity. I chose to feel sorry for the guards. They'd been brainwashed. They'd had their innocence stolen. They came to Auschwitz to throw children into a gas chamber, thinking they were ridding the world from a cancer. They'd lost their freedom. I still had mine.

A few months after our visit to Lausanne, Audrey returned to the International Institute of Management Development to give a workshop with Andreas at the High Performance Leadership program.

"We grew up on opposite sides of the transmission line of secrets and horror," Andreas said. Now they're collaborating to help today's business leaders focus on inner healing—to face the past and chart the course toward a better reality.

Among their students are Europeans, primarily from Germany and neighboring countries, who are in their thirties, forties, and fifties—a generation or two removed from WWII, curious about what happened in their families during the war. Other students are from places in Africa and southeastern Europe that have been ravaged by violence, who are figuring out how to face and release the tragedies their families have experienced—or inflicted. This workshop on inner healing, led by the daughter of a survivor and the grandson of a Nazi, is such a beautiful example of not only *how* to heal but *why*. For ourselves, and also for what our healing gives the world. For the new legacy we pass on.

"I used to participate in the silence about the past," Audrey said. "I was afraid of the pain." But she realized that in avoiding learning more she was holding on to grief. "Now I'd rather be curious," she said. "And I want to help."

Andreas agreed.

"It finally became clear to me why I invested so much time in the past," he said. "I think my ancestors would want corrective action to happen, insofar as it's possible. Realizing this, I'm much more at peace with them. I can stop questioning why they did what they did. I can focus on what I do now to contribute to peace."

We're born to love; we learn to hate. It's up to us what we reach for.

# KEYS TO FREE YOURSELF
# FROM JUDGMENT

- ***Our best teachers.*** *The most toxic, obnoxious people in our lives can be our best teachers. The next time you're in the presence of someone who irks or offends you, soften your eyes and tell yourself, "Human, no more, no less. Human, like me." Then ask, "What are you here to teach me?"*

- ***We're born to love; we learn to hate.*** *Make a list of the messages you heard growing up that divided people into categories: us/them; good/bad; right/wrong. Circle any of these messages that describe how you see the world today. Notice where you may be holding on to judgment. How is this judgment affecting your relationships? Is it limiting your choices or ability to take risks?*

- ***What's the legacy you want to pass on?*** *We can't choose what our ancestors did, or what was done to them. But we get to create the recipe that's handed down. Write a recipe for a life well-lived. Take the good things from your family's past and add your own ingredients. Give the next generation something delicious and nourishing to build on.*

# CHAPTER 11

# If I Survive
# Today, Tomorrow
# I Will Be Free

## The Prison of Hopelessness

In Auschwitz, I was haunted by a persistent thought: does anyone know Magda and I are here?

Any answer pointed to hopelessness. If people knew and didn't intervene, then what was the value of my life? And if no one knew, how would we ever get out?

When hopelessness overwhelmed me, I'd think of what my mother had told me in the dark, crowded cattle car on our way to prison: "We don't know where we're going. We don't know what's going to happen. Just remember, no one can take away what you've put in your mind."

During the long, terrible days and nights in prison, I'd choose what to hold in my mind. I'd think of my boyfriend, Eric, how our romance kindled at a time of war, how we'd go picnicking by the river, eating my mother's delicious fried chicken and potato salad, planning our future. I'd think of dancing with him in the dress my father had made just before we were forced out of our home—how I tested the dress to make sure I could dance in it, to make sure the skirt twirled, how Eric's hands rested against the thin suede belt at my waist. I'd think of the last words he said to me as he watched my transport leave the brick factory: "I'll never forget your eyes. I'll never forget your hands." And I'd picture our reunion, how we would melt into each other's arms with joy and relief. These thoughts were like a candle I held through the very darkest hours and months. It's not that daydreaming about Eric erased the horror. It didn't bring back my parents or ease the pain of their deaths—or the looming threat of my own. But thinking of him helped me see past where I was, to envision a tomorrow that included my beloved, to keep starvation and torture in perspective. I was living through hell on earth—and it was temporary. If it was temporary, it could be survived.

Hope really is a matter of life and death. I knew a young woman in Auschwitz who became certain that the camp would be liberated by Christmas. She'd seen the new arrivals dwindle, heard rumors that the Germans were facing major military losses, and convinced herself that it was only a matter of weeks before we'd be free. But then Christmas came and went. No one arrived to liberate the camp. The day after Christmas my friend was dead. Hope had kept her going. When her hope died, she did, too.

I was reminded of this more than seventy years later, in a hospital in La Jolla, a few months after the release of my first book, *The Choice*. For decades, it had been my dream to finally put my story of healing on the page, to encourage as many people as possible all over the world to embark on and continue the journey toward freedom. Lots of amazing and affirming things were happening—every day I received moving letters from readers, invitations to speak at conferences and special events and interviews with international media.

One exciting day, Deepak Chopra invited me to participate in a Facebook Live event he would be hosting at the Chopra Center in Carlsbad. I was thrilled. And because physical maintenance takes time at my age, I immediately went to work. I scheduled hair and makeup appointments so I'd look and feel my best; I pressed my favorite designer suit; and I tried to ignore the painful flares I kept feeling in my stomach, burning cramps that cried out for attention, like the jabs of hunger I'd experienced in Auschwitz. "Leave me alone," I told my tummy as I fixed my makeup. "I'm busy right now!"

I got up early the morning of the event and dressed carefully. As I adjusted my suit jacket in the mirror, I imagined my father watching me. "Look at me now!" I told him, smiling.

But when a friend came to pick me up to drive me to the Chopra Center, she found me hunched over, trying to ride another wave of terrible cramps. "I'm not taking you to the event," she said. "I'm taking you to the hospital."

I wouldn't hear of it. "It took me two days to get ready!" I said through gritted teeth. "I'm going to the Chopra Center." She drove there as fast as she could, and when we arrived, I hurried in, barely managing to greet Deepak and his wife before falling to my knees in the bathroom. I clutched the edge of the bowl, terrified I'd embarrass myself by making a mess on the floor, and then passed out from the pain. The next thing I knew, Deepak was holding my arms, guiding me back into the car, and I went straight to the hospital, where the doctors found that a part of my small intestine was twisted and needed to be resected. I would need surgery immediately. "If you'd waited an hour longer," the surgeon said, "you'd be dead."

When I woke up from the operation hours later, groggy and numb, the nurses told me I was the most elegant patient they'd ever seen coming out of the operating room. Apparently, my makeup was still perfect.

I didn't feel elegant. I felt like a helpless infant—delirious with medications, unable to make sense of my surroundings, and unable to move without assistance. I had to push a button for someone to take me to the bathroom and then would wait in fear that a nurse or medical assistant wouldn't arrive in time. I didn't feel fully human. I felt reduced to a collection of basic needs— hunger, thirst, elimination—and was incapable of meeting them myself.

Worst of all, I was intubated and couldn't speak. To be helpless *and* voiceless brought back too many horrible memories. I grabbed at the tube, tried to pull it out. The nurses were worried I'd suffocate myself and tied my hands down. Now I was truly terrified. My automatic physical reactions—PTSD symptoms— brought on by the trauma of my past meant that I couldn't stand being confined. Tight spaces, anything holding me down sent me into panic. My heart raced dangerously fast, contracting before it could fill with blood. Tied down and mute in the hospital, I felt that to continue living was too steep a feat.

My three beautiful children—Marianne, Audrey, and John— had been by my side since the surgery and tirelessly advocating on my behalf, ensuring my medications were adjusted to keep me as lucid as possible, rubbing my favorite Chanel lotion into my parched skin. My grandchildren visited. Rachel and Audrey brought me a soft robe. They were all taking such good care of me, doing all they could to offer dignity and comfort. But I was hooked up to so many machines. Would I ever be able to function again without them? I didn't want to be kept breathing if I couldn't fully live. Once my hands were free, I gestured for Marianne to bring me a piece of paper and a pen. *I want to die—happy*, I scrawled.

They reassured me that they'd let me go when it was time, and Marianne pocketed my note. They didn't seem to understand that I was ready to go *now*. Later that day Dr. McCaul, my lung doctor, came through on his rounds and said I was looking good. He'd take the tube out the next day, he promised. My children smiled and kissed me. "See, Mom," they said. "You're going to be fine." As the long hours of the afternoon ticked by, and all my monitors and support machines beeped and clicked around me, I tried to convince myself. *It's temporary*, I told myself. *I can survive this*. I dozed and woke up more times than I can count, and then passed a restless, endless night staring out the little square window of the hospital room, sleeping and waking again. The sun rose. I'd made it after all. The tube would come out that day.

*It's temporary*, I repeated, waiting for Dr. McCaul to come and remove the tube. *It's temporary*. But when the doctor arrived, he paused, double-checked his notes, and then sighed. "I think we need to give it another day."

I wasn't able to speak to tell him that I didn't have another day in me. Not understanding how close I was to giving up, he gave me a reassuring smile and went about his rounds.

I woke up deep in the middle of that night. My whole body was curled inward, shutting out the world. I wondered if this was what it felt like to finally let go. Then I heard an inner voice: "You did it in Auschwitz. You can do it again now." I had a choice. I could give in and give up. Or I could choose hope. A new feeling washed through my body. I felt three generations—my children, grandchildren, and great-grandchildren—gathering to buoy me up. I thought of Marianne jumping for joy when she visited me in the hospital after Audrey was born, shouting, "I got my sister! I got my sister!" John, whose childhood difficulties taught me that no matter what happens, we never give up. Lindsey's glowing face when she became a mom. My great-grandson Hale's sweet voice calling me Gi-Gi Baby. David as a toddler lifting up his shirt so I could kiss his belly button, crying, "Do me! Do me!" Jordan as a teenager acting tough with his friends, then asking for warm milk and honey at bedtime. Rachel's beautiful eyes gazing at me just that morning as she massaged my feet. I had to live, because I never wanted to stop looking into those eyes! I felt the gift of all of them, the gift of life. The pain and fatigue weren't gone, but my limbs and heart felt alive, thrumming with the call of possibility and purpose, with the realization that I wasn't done helping others, that there was more here on this planet that I wanted to do.

When it's our time, it's our time. We can't choose when we die. But I no longer wanted to. I wanted to live.

The next day, the doctor came back, the tube came out, and Audrey helped me walk down the hall, pulling all the medication drips and machines along with us. Nurses lined the hallway, cheering me on, clapping, amazed to see me out of bed, determined to walk no matter how much equipment I had to drag with me. Within a week, I was home. When I was strapped in the hospital bed and chose hope, I didn't know that in a year I'd get an email from Oprah saying that she'd read my book and wanted to interview me on *SuperSoul Sunday*.

We never know what's ahead. Hope isn't the white paint we use to mask our suffering. It's an investment in curiosity. A recognition that if we give up now, we'll never get to see what happens next.

I thought nothing in my life would surpass the happiness I felt when I found out I was pregnant with my first child. My doctor cautioned me against continuing the pregnancy, afraid I wasn't physically strong enough to grow a healthy baby or endure child-birth, but I skipped through the streets after the appointment, barely able to contain my joy that after so much suffering and senseless death I would carry life into the world. I celebrated by eating as much rye bread and raw potato spaetzle as I could hold. I grinned at my reflection in shop windows. I put on fifty pounds.

**CHOOSING HOPE AFFECTS WHAT GETS MY ATTENTION EVERY DAY.**

In the decades since Marianne's birth, there's much I've gained and lost and almost lost. All of it has taught me how much I have, and how to celebrate each precious moment, without waiting for someone else's permission or approval. I am reminded again and again: to choose hope is to choose life.

Hope does not guarantee anything about what will happen in the future. The scoliosis I've had since the war has stayed with me. It affects my lung, pushing it closer and closer to my heart. I don't know if I'll have a heart attack, or when I might wake up unable to breathe.

But choosing hope affects what gets my attention every day. I can think young. I can choose what I do to fill my day with passion—to dance and do the high kick as long as I'm able; to reread books that are meaningful to me, and go to movies and the opera and theater; to savor good food and high fashion; to spend time with people who are kind and have integrity; to remember that loss and trauma don't mean you have to stop living fully.

"You've seen firsthand the greatest evils of the world," people say. "How can you hold hope when there's still genocide in the world, when there's so much evidence to the contrary?"

To ask how hope is possible in the face of dire realities is to confuse hope with idealism. Idealism is when you expect that everything in life is going to be fair or good or easy. It's a defense mechanism, just like denial or delusion.

Honey, don't cover garlic with chocolate. It doesn't taste good. Likewise, there's no freedom in denying reality, or trying to cloak it in something sweet. Hope isn't a distraction from darkness. It's a confrontation *with* darkness.

Shortly after I began writing this book, I happened upon a TV interview with Ben Ferencz, who at ninety-nine years old is the last living person to have prosecuted Nazis at Nuremberg, essentially the biggest murder trial the world has ever known.

Ferencz was only twenty-seven at the time. The son of Jewish Romanian immigrant parents, he served in the US Army during World War II, fighting in the Normandy invasion and the Battle of the Bulge. Then, as the concentration camps were being liberated, he was sent in to gather evidence. Traumatized by what he saw, he vowed never to return to Germany.

He went home to New York and was just preparing to begin practicing law when he was recruited to go to Berlin to investigate

Nazi offices and archives for evidence to aid the prosecution of the Nuremberg war crimes trials. As he catalogued Nazi documents, he discovered reports written by the Einsatzgruppen, SS units deployed as killing squads. The reports listed numbers of men, women, and children shot in cold blood in towns and villages all over Nazi-occupied Europe. Ferencz added up the number of dead: more than one million, slaughtered at home, buried in mass graves.

"Seventy-one years later," Ferencz said, "and I'm still churning."

This is where hope comes in. If he'd clung to idealism, he would have tried to forget the excruciating truth, or buried it in wishful thinking—the war's over, the world is better now, it won't happen again. If he'd lost himself to hopelessness, he would have said, "Humanity is ugly. Nothing can be done." But Ferencz reached for hope. He determined to do everything in his power to affirm the rule of law, to deter similar crimes from ever being committed again, and was appointed chief prosecutor for the United States in the Einsatzgruppen case. He was only twenty-seven. It was his first trial.

**HOPE IS CURIOSITY WRIT LARGE.**

He's been alive for close to a century, and he continues to advocate for peace and social justice.

"It takes courage not to be discouraged," he said. But never give up, he reminds us. There's progress and change all around us—and nothing new ever happened before.

I remembered his words when I spoke recently in Rancho Santa Fe, a formerly segregated community north of San Diego where, not that long ago, Jews weren't allowed to live. Now the community is celebrating the fifteenth anniversary of welcoming Rancho Santa Fe's first Chabad rabbi.

If we decide something's hopeless or impossible, it will be. If we take action, who knows what we might manifest? Hope is curiosity writ large. A willingness to cultivate within yourself whatever kindles light, and to shine that light into the darkest places.

Hope is the boldest act of imagination I know.

Seeds of despair abound.

I survived Auschwitz and Communist Europe and came to America, land of the free, and discovered that the bathrooms and drinking fountains in the factory where I worked in Baltimore were segregated. I'd fled hate and prejudice, only to find more prejudice and hate.

A few months after I started working on this book, on the last day of Passover, the Jewish holiday celebrating liberation, an armed man walked into an Orthodox synagogue near San Diego, where I live, and opened fire, killing one congregant. He said, "I'm just trying to defend my nation from the Jewish people." A few months later, in a Walmart in El Paso, Texas, my former home, another young white man shot and killed twenty-two people in a murderous act of anti-immigrant, white-supremacist hate. Did my parents die so the past could be repeated?

I'll never forget the lurch in my gut when I finished a lecture for a university class in El Paso many years ago, and the professor asked, "How many of you know about Auschwitz?" There were at least two hundred people in that auditorium. Only five students raised their hands.

Ignorance is the enemy of hope.

And it's the *catalyst* for hope.

I had the privilege of meeting one of the survivors of the San Diego synagogue shooting a few weeks before he started his first year of college. Born in Israel, he had immigrated to the United States with his family when he was nine. His parents weren't strongly religious, but he and his father had recently started attending synagogue every Saturday, a practice he found helpful "to think, reboot, refresh, sort of reflect on what I did wrong and right during the week." The morning of the shooting he was also trying to decide which college to attend, weighing his options. While his father stayed in the sanctuary to hear the reading of the Torah, he sat in the front foyer of the synagogue, his favorite spot to pray and reflect. He was gazing out the window, when out of the corner of his eye he saw a man enter the building, then the tip of a gun, bullets flying, a woman falling to the ground. "Run!" he told himself. He jumped up to flee, but the gunman noticed and ran after him, yelling, "You'd better run, motherfucker!" He found an empty room, dove under a desk, pressed himself to the wood. The gunman's footsteps reached the doorway. My young friend held his breath. The footsteps retreated. My friend didn't dare move. He was still pressed against the desk, trying not to breathe, when his father found him. The gunman had fled the building, his father reassured him. But he remained frozen under the desk.

"I'm going to speak to you, survivor to survivor," I told him. "This experience is always going to be with you." I told him the flashbacks and panic usually don't go away. But what we call

> IGNORANCE IS THE ENEMY OF HOPE. AND IT'S THE CATALYST FOR HOPE.

post-traumatic stress disorder is not a disorder—it's a very normal reaction to loss, violence, and tragedy. Though he'll never overcome what he witnessed that day, he can come to terms with it. Even use it, as we can use everything in life, to fuel our growth and purpose.

That's the hope I offer you.

You could have died, too, somehow. Perhaps there've been times when you've wanted to. But you didn't. Hope is the conviction that you survived all that you survived so that you can be a good role model. An ambassador for freedom. A person who focuses not on what you've lost, but on what's still here for you, on the work you're called to do.

There's always something to do.

My aunt Matilda, who lived to be one hundred, woke up every morning and said, "It could be worse, and it could be better." That's how she started each day. I'm ninety-two, and most days I wake up and feel some kind of pain. That's reality. It's part of aging, part of living with scoliosis and damaged lungs. The day I feel no pain is the day I'm dead.

Hope doesn't obscure or whitewash reality. Hope tells us that life is full of darkness and suffering—and yet if we survive today, tomorrow we'll be free.

# KEYS TO FREE YOURSELF FROM HOPELESSNESS

- ***Don't cover garlic with chocolate.*** *It's tempting to confuse hope with idealism, but idealism is just another form of denial, a way of evading a true confrontation with suffering. Resiliency and freedom don't come from pretending away our pain. Listen to the way you talk about a hard or hurtful situation.* It's okay. It's not that bad. Others have it so much worse. I don't have anything to complain about. Everything will work out in the end. No pain, no glory! *The next time you hear yourself using the language of minimization, delusion, or denial, try replacing the words with: "It hurts. And it's temporary." Remind yourself, "I've survived pain before."*

- ***It takes courage not to be discouraged.*** *There's progress and change all around us; nothing new ever happened before. Set a timer for ten minutes and make a list of as many things as you can think of that are better now than they were five years ago. Think on the global scale—human rights advances, technological innovations, new works of art. And think on the personal level—things you've made, achieved, or changed for the better. Let the work that still needs doing be a catalyst for hope, not despair.*

- ***Hope is an investment in curiosity.*** *Find a comfortable seat or lie down and close your eyes. Relax your body. Take a few centering breaths. Imagine yourself walking along a path or a road. You're on your way to meet your future* *self. Where are you walking? Along a bright city street? In a forest? Along a country lane? Notice your surroundings in vivid sensory detail—pay attention to sights, smells, sounds, tastes, and physical sensations. Now you're arriving at your future self's doorstep. Where does your future self live? In a skyscraper? Log cabin? House with a wide front porch? The door opens. Your future self greets you. What does your future self look like? What is he or she wearing? Embrace or shake hands. Then ask, "What is it you want me to know?"*

# CHAPTER 12

# There's No Forgiveness Without Rage

## The Prison of Not Forgiving

People often ask how I can ever forgive the Nazis. I don't have the godly power to anoint anyone with forgiveness, to spiritually cleanse others for their wrongs.

But I have the power to free myself.

So do you.

Forgiveness isn't something we do for the person who's hurt us. It's something we do for ourselves, so we're no longer victims or prisoners of the past, so we can stop carrying a burden that harbors nothing but pain.

Another misconception about forgiveness is that the way to make peace with someone who has harmed us is to say, "I'm done with her."

It doesn't work that way. It's not about cutting someone out. It's about letting go.

As long as you say you can't forgive someone, you're spending energy being *against* rather than being *for* yourself and the life you deserve. To forgive isn't to give someone permission to keep hurting you. It's not okay that you were harmed. But it's already done. No one but you can heal the wound.

This kind of release doesn't come easily. It's not an overnight process. And lots of things get in the way. A desire for justice, or revenge, an apology, even just acknowledgment.

For years I maintained the fantasy of tracking down Josef Mengele in Paraguay, where he fled after the war. I'd pose as a sympathizer, a journalist, to gain access, and then I'd walk into his house and look him in the face and say, "I'm the girl who danced for you in Auschwitz. You murdered my mother." I wanted to see the look on his face, the truth land in his eyes, no place to run. I wanted him to stand before his wrongs, defenseless. I wanted to feel strong and triumphant because he was weak. I wasn't after revenge, not exactly. Somehow I sensed that making someone else hurt wasn't going to take away my pain. But for a long time, this fantasy gave me such satisfaction. Except that it didn't take away my rage and grief—it just deferred them.

It's easier to release the past when others see your truth, tell the truth. When there's a collective process—restorative justice, war crimes tribunals, truth and reconciliation committees—through which perpetrators are accountable for the harm they inflicted and the court of the world holds the truth to the light.

But *your* life doesn't depend on what you get or don't get from someone else. Your life is your own.

What I say next might surprise you.

There's no forgiveness without rage.

For many years I had tremendous problems with anger. I wouldn't acknowledge it. It terrified me. I thought that I'd get lost in it. That once it started, it was never going to end. That it would totally consume me. But as I've said before, the opposite of depression is expression. What comes out of our body doesn't make us ill. What stays in there does. Forgiveness is release, and I couldn't let go until I gave myself permission to feel and express my rage. I finally asked my therapist to sit on me, to hold me down so I had a force to push against, so I could release a primal scream.

> SILENT RAGE IS SELF-DESTRUCTIVE.

Silent rage is self-destructive. If you're not actively, consciously, intentionally releasing it, you're holding on to it. And that's not going to do you any good.

Neither is venting anger. That's when you blow your top. It might feel cathartic in the moment, but others foot the bill. And it can become addictive. You're not really releasing anything. You're just perpetuating a cycle—a harmful one.

The best thing to do with anger is to learn to channel it, and then dissolve it.

It might sound simple enough. But if you've been taught to be a "good girl" or a "good boy," taught that anger is unacceptable or frightening, if you've been hurt by someone else's rage, it isn't easy to let yourself feel—much less express—your anger.

When Lena's husband suddenly told her with no explanation, no discussion, that he wanted a divorce, she was shocked by loss. A year later, she's coping admirably, staying on top of work, supporting and loving her three kids, even beginning to date again, sporting a chic haircut and bold earrings. Yet she feels stuck on the inside, unable to move past the feeling that she's been cheated by life.

"I lost something I didn't want to lose," she said. "I wasn't given a choice." She went through feelings of deep sadness, grief, and guilt. She summoned strength and energy she didn't know she had to support her children, proceed with the pragmatic matters of the divorce. But through it all, she couldn't feel any anger. She'd witnessed a favorite aunt go through a similarly rattling divorce many years earlier, had watched her aunt recede from the world, holding her breath for decades, waiting for her ex-husband to realize he'd made a mistake and beg to come back. She'd died of cancer, still waiting for her husband to return. Haunted by her aunt's sorrow, Lena took herself for a walk in the woods one day, wanting to release the rage she knew must be lurking within, even if she couldn't feel it. She followed a trail deep into the forest, and stood among the trees, all alone, prepared to let herself scream as loudly as she could. But the scream wouldn't come. She was blocked. The more she tried to embrace her anger, the more numb she felt.

"How can I feel and express my anger?" she asked me. "I'm so scared of feeling it. I don't want to feel it."

"First, legitimize it," I told her.

You have a right to feel rage. It's a human emotion. You are human.

When we can't release anger, we're either denying that we were victimized, or denying that we're human. (That's how a perfectionist suffers. Silently!) Either way, we're denying reality. Making ourselves numb, pretending to be fine.

This doesn't set you free.

Scream and pound your fists into a pillow. Go to a beach or mountaintop alone and yell into the wind. Grab a giant stick, smash and beat the ground. We sing alone in the car. Why not scream alone? Roll up all the windows, take a giant breath, and when you exhale, give it voice, let it crescendo into the world's longest and loudest scream. When a patient comes to see me, looking rigid or masked, I say, "I feel like screaming today. Shall we scream?" And we do it together. If you're afraid to scream alone, find a friend or therapist to scream with you. It's such a release! And it's so profound, even exhilarating, to hear your own unadulterated voice, charged with feeling, expressing its most difficult truth. To hear yourself unmasked. To stand up, claim your space, say, "I was victimized, but I'm not a victim. I am me."

Anger is a secondary emotion, a defense, armor we put up around the primary feeling underneath. We burn through anger so we can get to what's underneath: fear or grief.

Only then can we begin the hardest work of all.

Forgiving ourselves.

One Friday afternoon in August, shortly after I'd started drafting chapters for this book, I came home to find a man at my front door.

He was dressed in khakis and a polo shirt, an official-looking ID badge clipped to his chest.

"I'm here from the water company," he said. "I have to check your water for contamination."

I let him inside, brought him to the kitchen. He turned the water on, checked the faucets in the bathrooms, and then told me, "I need to call in my supervisor, we could have a problem with metals." He used his cell phone to bring in a colleague for support.

A man wearing the same outfit and badge arrived, they tried all the faucets again, and then told me I'd need to remove anything on my body that was metal. Watches, belts, jewelry. I took off my necklace and bracelet. The rings were more difficult. Because of my arthritis, my rings have been modified with little pins so I can unclasp them, otherwise I'd never be able to slide them over my swollen joints. But arthritis also makes it difficult to pull the pins. I asked the men to help me.

They tested the faucets again and performed some kind of treatment on the water. Go to the bathroom sink, they told me, and run the water until it turns blue. I walked down the hall, turned the water on, watched it flow, waited and waited. Then I knew. I hurried back to the kitchen, but they were already gone—along with my necklace and bracelet and rings.

The police said I'd been the latest target of a well-known elder abuse scheme. I felt so foolish and gullible to have been taken in by the ruse. I cringed every time I thought of how stupid and trusting I'd been. I let them in, I let them walk through my house, I handed them my jewelry. I might as well have written them a check!

The police—and my children—see it differently. Thank

goodness you obeyed, they say. They took things, but they didn't hurt me. If I'd tried to resist, they could have tied me up, or worse. Doing everything they asked without a fuss might have saved my life.

This perspective is helpful. But it doesn't take the feelings away.

The loss of things I've valued and held dear—especially the bracelet, the one Béla gave me to celebrate Marianne's birth, that I'd smuggled out of Czechoslovakia by hiding it in her diaper. It's just an object, yet it stands for something more, for life, motherhood, freedom—all things worth celebrating and fighting for. My arm feels naked without it.

Then there was fear. For days I had an obsessive feeling that they were going to come back and kill me so I wouldn't talk.

Then there was the desire to chew out the criminals, to punish them, diminish them. "Is this how your mother raised you to be?" I imagined yelling. "Aren't you ashamed?"

And then there was *my* shame. *I* opened the door. I answered their questions. I followed their commands, held out my hand so they could unclasp my ring. I hated the version of me that I saw. Vulnerable. Frail. Gullible.

But the only one putting those labels on me was me.

What I'm saying is that life keeps giving me opportunities to choose freedom—to love myself as I am: human, imperfect, and whole. So I forgave myself, releasing them so I can release me.

I have life to live and work to do and love to share. I don't have time to hold on to the fear or anger or shame anymore, to give anything else to two people who already stole something from me. I won't give them another inch. I won't hand my power away.

* * *

During my recent visit to Europe, Audrey and I went to Amsterdam, where I spoke at the Anne Frank House, and then was honored in the most spectacular way. Igone de Jongh, the prima ballerina of the Dutch National Ballet, choreographed and performed a piece inspired by my first night in Auschwitz when I danced for Mengele.

The performance was on May 4, 2019, the seventy-fourth anniversary of my liberation at Gunskirchen, and a day of national remembrance in the Netherlands. The whole country observes two minutes of silence in honor of those who died in the camps and those who survived. When Audrey and I arrived at the theater, we were welcomed like celebrities, applauded, given flowers. People wept and embraced us. The king and queen were late to the performance, and we were offered their seats.

The performance itself was one of the most exquisite and cherished experiences of my life. I was completely overwhelmed by the strength, grace, and passion of Igone de Jongh, by the depiction of beauty and transcendence—in hell. Even more overwhelming was the portrayal of Mengele. He was a hungry ghost, sad and empty, approaching and approaching me, his prisoner, but never fulfilled, trapped by his need for power and control.

The performers took their bows and the audience rose in thunderous applause. Just as the clapping was beginning to die down, Igone de Jongh, her arms full of flowers, came down from the stage and walked directly to where Audrey and I were sitting. A spotlight beamed down on us. The ballerina embraced me, tears in her eyes, and then gave me her biggest bouquet. The theater exploded in emotion. I couldn't see to walk when we left our seats, my eyes still too full of tears.

It took me so many years to work through my anger and grief, to release Mengele and Hitler, to forgive myself for having survived. But in the theater with my daughter, watching one of the darkest moments of my past brought to life on the stage, I knew again what I realized that night in the barracks—that while Mengele had all the power, while day after day he chose with his grotesquely wagging finger who would live and who would die, he was more a prisoner than I was.

I was innocent.

And free.

## KEYS TO FREE YOURSELF
## FROM NOT FORGIVING

- *Am I ready to forgive?* *Think of a person who has wronged or harmed you. Do any of these statements ring true?* What she did was unforgivable. He hasn't earned my forgiveness. I'm ready to give her the gift of my forgiveness. If I forgive, I'll let him off the hook. If I forgive, I'll give him permission to keep hurting me. I'll forgive once there's justice, or an apology or acknowledgment. *If you relate to one or more of these statements, you are likely spending energy being against someone, rather than for yourself and the life you deserve. Forgiveness isn't something you give someone else. It's how you release yourself.*

- *Acknowledge and release rage.* *Make a rage date with yourself. If the idea of being angry is too terrifying to face alone, ask a trusted friend or therapist to help you. Legitimize your anger, then choose a way to channel and then dissolve it. Scream and yell. Hit a punching bag. Bang the ground with a stick. Break plates on the patio. Get the rage moving, let it out so it doesn't fester and contaminate you. Don't stop until there's nothing left. In a day or a week, do it again.*

- *Forgive yourself.* *If I'm having trouble releasing someone who has hurt me, it may be that I'm holding on to guilt or shame or judgment toward myself. We're born innocent. Imagine you're holding a precious baby in your arms. Feel the warmth and trust of this tiny being. Gaze into the curious, wide-open eyes, at the little hands that reach as though to take in every detail of the whole, unfathomable, bountiful world. This baby is you. Say, "I'm here. I live for you."*

# CONCLUSION

# The Gift

We can't take away suffering, we can't change what happened—but we can choose to find the gift in our lives. We can even learn to cherish the wound.

There's a Hungarian adage that says you find the darkest shadow beneath the candle. Our darkest and brightest places—our shadows and our flames—are intertwined. My most terrifying night, the first one in Auschwitz, taught me a vital lesson that has enhanced and empowered my life ever since. The very worst circumstances gave me the opportunity to discover the inner resources that helped me again and again to survive. My years of introspection, of being alone and working hard as a ballet student and gymnast, helped me survive hell; and hell taught me to keep dancing for my life.

Life—even with its inevitable trauma, pain, grief, misery, and death—is a gift. A gift we sabotage when we imprison ourselves in our fears of punishment, failure, and abandonment; in our need for approval; in shame and blame; in superiority and inferiority; in our need for power and control. To celebrate the gift of life is to find the gift in everything that happens, even the parts that are difficult, that we're not sure we can survive. To celebrate life, period. To live with joy, love, and passion.

Sometimes we think that if we move on from loss or trauma, if we have fun and enjoy ourselves, if we continue to grow and evolve, that we're somehow dishonoring the dead, or dishonoring the past. But it's okay to laugh! It's okay to have joy! Even in Auschwitz we were celebrating in our minds all the time, cooking feasts, arguing over how much caraway you put in the best rye bread, how much paprika in Hungarian chicken paprikash. We even held a boob contest one night! (Guess who won?)

I can't say that everything happens for a reason, that there's a purpose in injustice or suffering. But I can say that pain, hardship, and suffering are the gift that helps us grow and learn and become who we are meant to be.

During the final days of the war, we were starving to death and cannibalism broke out in the camp. I was immobile on the muddy ground, hallucinating with hunger, praying for a way to keep living without succumbing to eating human flesh. And a voice said, "There's grass to eat." Even at death's door, I had a choice. I could choose which blade of grass to eat.

I used to ask, "Why me?" But now I ask, "Why *not* me?" Perhaps I survived so I can choose what to do with what happened, and how to be here now. So I can show others how to choose life, so my parents and all the innocents didn't die in vain. So I can turn all the lessons I learned in hell into a gift I offer you now: the opportunity to decide what kind of life you want to have, to discover the untapped potential lying in the shadows, to reveal and reclaim who you really are.

Honey, may you also choose to give up the prison and do the work to be free. To find in your suffering your own life lessons. To choose which legacy the world inherits. To hand down the pain—or to pass on the gift.

# AFTERWORD

*April, 2021*

In the year since I finished writing *The Gift,* we have experienced a global pandemic that has asked us, over and over again, to do just as well as we can. We've been forced into a difficult and ongoing limbo, a long-term relationship with the unexpected and the unanticipated. Each one of us has experienced fear, uncertainty, and loss of some kind. We've had to adapt our everyday lives in considerable ways. We didn't know—and we still don't know—what's going to happen next.

When my life was interrupted by war, I was a young girl in love. I wanted to be a ballerina. I had no idea that such a place as a death camp existed, much less that I'd be a prisoner there. I never would have expected that I'd come to America, or become a psychologist. The other day, as I did the high kick at the end of a Zoom presentation to a lovely audience in Brazil, I suddenly thought, *Here I am. I made it.* I'm not what I once thought I'd be. Yet I embrace the life that I have, the survivor I've become.

I've said before that Auschwitz was ultimately a place of discovery. Perhaps this year has helped you discover something too—to find your strength to grow and endure, to become aware of the parts of you that you never knew were possible, to leave behind the old roles you played to become the person you truly are.

My loved ones were worried about me during lockdown, both for my physical and mental health. My lungs are vulnerable, which makes Covid-19 a particularly threatening virus. And they were concerned that the fear and isolation might aggravate my PTSD symptoms. But I've found this year that I don't panic as easily as I used to. With so much uncertainty, I choose to focus on the constants in my life—on what I *do* have, on my love for my family, patients, and friends. And with daily life pared down to the essentials, I choose to let go of what isn't as important as I once thought, and embrace what really matters. I've also discovered some interesting surprises. Outside of my clinical work, connecting with local and global audiences is my primary purpose in life, and I was upset and disappointed not to be able to travel to speaking engagements. But I've found that life on digital platforms has actually made it easier for me to engage with people all over the world. I love Zoom—I don't have to get dressed or leave my house, I just put on a new scarf and sit down! I've been busier and more connected than ever before.

While the pain of this year is real and not to be discounted, while we gain nothing by minimizing our anger or our grief, there have been unexpected gifts of pandemic life. It's like the coach has called a long time-out, and as the world begins to open up again, we have a chance to regroup and redecide: What gets our time and attention? What choices do we have right now, and in every moment, to harness the freedom within?

**If you're not happy alone you won't be happy with anyone.**
Many of us have spent unprecedented amounts of time alone
this year, in our own company. While the isolation has been
challenging, even devastating, it's also an opportunity to know
ourselves more fully, to accept and love ourselves more.

Before the pandemic, what were your habitual distractions?
How did you keep busy? What happened when you had to stop
doing these things, when you had no escape from the discomfort
of being with yourself?

You're the only one you have for a lifetime. Marriages and
romantic relationships may end. Children grow up and move
away. Dear friends may die. You are your only constant. Now
it's time to give birth to the genuine self you might have had to
give up to pay the bills or please someone else. What about your
own company do you most enjoy? In what ways can you always
rely on yourself? How do you express your love and gratitude for
your own most precious companion—you?

**Whatever you practice you get good at.** This is a good time
to think about your thinking, to pay attention to what you're
paying attention to, because that's what you'll reinforce. If
you're full of guilt, worry, and fear, you're going to have more
guilt, worry, and fear. And guilt is in the past; worry is in the
future. Our freedom lies in our power to choose what we do
*in the present.*

You can't choose what happens to you, or what others say or
do—but you can take charge of your thinking, feeling, and behavior. It's especially important to notice how you talk to yourself. To
listen to your inner dialogue. Is it full of words like *always, never,
should,* and *have to*? Is it full of self-love, or self-hate? How can

you speak to yourself so you become your own loving parent, your own best cheerleader?

I like to wake up in the morning, meet my own eyes in the mirror, and say, "Love you." I like to go about my day saying, "Yes I am, yes I can, yes I will!"

**Become child-like, not childish.** We all have a little child in us, the one who wants something because she wants it. This year has taught us to distinguish between our needs and our wants.

Instead of demanding that the world be the way you want it to be, how can you bring your open-eyed curiosity on board? How can you drop your agenda and see what's really here, right in front of you?

Each one of us is born a seed; whatever happens to us is our fertilizer. What about this year has helped you grow toward the light?

**The problem with understanding.** Life isn't easy, and sometimes things don't go our way. Often, we try to protect ourselves and regain control by trying to understand why something is happening. But how can I ever *understand* that Dr. Mengele separated me from my mother in the selection line, telling me, "You'll see your mother very soon. She's just going to take a shower"? How can I *understand* that my parents died and I lived?

There's a lot about the pandemic we'll never understand. It's not our job to keep figuring and figuring, and digging and digging, trying to discover *why this* or *why that*. It keeps us stuck in the past.

We can stop fighting or running away from our circumstances and simply say, "I don't like it. It's inconvenient." And we can stop avoiding reality by denying or minimizing what's happening. It's okay to be angry. Use your rage as a trigger to ask, "How can I be useful? How can I show up right now? Is this the best I can do?"

**"Don't be too happy in the morning because you might cry at night,"** I've heard people say. In a climate of constant uncertainty, it's tempting to be cautious with our joy; to hold our breath, wait for the other shoe to drop. Anticipating disaster can give us an illusion of control. But it doesn't make us free.

In Auschwitz, where nothing came from the outside, we could transcend our physical prison by becoming free in our minds. We would imagine feasts, cooking and savoring dish after dish, moving our focus from the consuming hunger in our bellies to the nourishment available within.

No matter what's happening on the outside, there's always a way to let joy and beauty into your life. The other day, a friend of mine brought me osso buco, a lovely stew of veal shanks, white wine, tomatoes, and carrots, from my favorite Italian restaurant. I ate half, and saved the rest to eat later. What tastes can you savor today? What kindness from a stranger or a friend? What delicious morsel can you tuck away for tomorrow?

As my mother told me in the cattle car on the way to Auschwitz, "No one can take away from you what you put in your own mind." Your gratitude, your memories, your storehouse of pleasures—these are yours to keep.

**We're born with two ears, and one mouth.** When I was a high school psychology teacher, my students and I did an experiment to test how well people really listen to one another. For a whole day, if someone gave us a generic greeting like, "Hi, how are you?" we'd reply in a neutral tone, "My mother died this morning." We discovered that most of the time, the person didn't really hear what we'd said. They'd reply with a rote, "Great to see you," or, "Have a good one." It was unsettling to recognize that many of us go about our lives hearing but not listening, exchanging words but not really communicating.

If we're on auto-pilot, we're not really living. The unexpected is useful because even if it's unpleasant, it shakes us out of our habits and assumptions. It helps us pay attention. In what ways has the pandemic made you a better listener? What have you noticed this year that you weren't in the habit of noticing before? How can you tune into your body and your heart now, and become a better listener to yourself?

**My favorite four-letter words are T-I-M-E and R-I-S-K.** Time, because in choosing how to spend it, we have the opportunity to find a balance between working, playing, and loving, and decide how we want to show up for others—and ourselves.

And risk, because it's through taking risks that we grow. Hazards hurt and threaten us, but risks stretch our comfort zone, giving us an opportunity to discover the part in us that is able to endure what we can't control, to say, "This is temporary, and I can survive it."

Everything in life is temporary. So what can you do today that you previously avoided? How can you turn your anxiety into excitement? And how can you discern not only what feeds you, but what truly nourishes you? Today, say no to one thing that depletes you; say yes to one thing that empowers you.

**There's no going back.** When I immigrated from Europe to America and our ship was crossing the English Channel, we came upon a storm and had to reroute. I remember the tugging feeling in my gut as the huge ship changed direction, my fear that we'd get off course, that we'd never reach our destination, that we'd be left eternally revolving in the churning sea. But the skipper took us around the storm and brought us back on track.

This year has thrown up obstacles and required detours. But we don't have to sacrifice our larger goals. The past is past. So where are you now, and where do you want to go? Freedom isn't about what you're *not* going to do, but what you *are* going to do. What do you stand for? What kind of life and habits do you want to build? What arrow are you following? Is it the one that takes you closer to our goals?

One of my first losses of the pandemic was not being able to gather with my family to celebrate Passover, a ritual that has special significance to me because Passover seder was the last meal my parents and sister and I shared in our home in Kassa, Hungary, in 1944. The next morning, we woke before dawn to the *nyilas*, the Hungarian Nazis, banging on our door. They rounded up all the Jewish families and drove us to the brick factory on the outskirts of town where we lived for a few weeks with little to eat, sleeping on the ground, before we were loaded into the cattle cars that brought us to Auschwitz. Every year I relive that last Passover with my parents, when I didn't know how brutally our lives would change, or that in a matter of weeks my parents would be dead.

I also reflect on the constant work of freedom, how we encounter many narrow places in our lives—oppressive or traumatic circumstances, nagging doubts, worries, and fears—and how we always get to choose how we respond, to find the Promised Land within.

Just a few weeks ago, my family gathered in my home for seder dinner. My daughters, Marianne and Audrey, came, and my niece, Ilona. Lindsey and Jordan, my grandchildren, were there with their children, my five great-grandsons—the one-year-old twins, born at the beginning of lockdown, were taking their first teetering steps, falling down and getting up, falling down and getting up. It was beautiful to see them taking risks, regaining their balance. That's how we all grow. In keeping with the spirit of adaptation we've all been practicing this year, we decided to do our seder differently—we did it backwards, starting with the meal, homemade matzo ball soup, chicken paprikash. It was the best seder yet.

At the end of the seder it's traditional to say, "Next year in Jerusalem." It's a way to honor the ongoing work of freedom, and our enduring hope that all may build a better and freer life. We are constantly in the process of renewing and becoming. This renewal starts with treating each day of life as a gift. And honoring that we're here because our ancestors didn't give up.

It's important to give yourself credit too.

Whatever you did, you made it. You didn't give up. You came closer to the dark, and you became stronger for it. Now seize your new beginning.

# ACKNOWLEDGMENTS

People don't come to me, I always say. They're sent to me.

I've been blessed by the contributions of countless wonderful people who've been sent to me. It's impossible to name every person who has moved, inspired, and taken care of me, thus contributing directly or indirectly to the creation of this book. To all of you who have touched my life, had faith in me, guided me not to give up—I celebrate your one-of-a-kind gifts and cherish your presence in my life. Thank you for replenishing my basket, helping me face the unknown, cope with the unanticipated and unexpected, and take responsibility for my life and my freedom.

To my patients, who inspire me never to retire, thank you for the ways you question me and teach me to be a good guide. And to the many people around the globe who have found meaning in my work, and especially to those who have told me their stories, thank you for moving me to share these lessons so that we all may greet each day full of passion for life—so that we all may be free.

To my teachers and mentors and all who have supported me to become a member of the healing arts profession, and to those who continue the work of guiding others, thank you for the ways you lead by example—taking care of yourselves while also moving beyond the "me," contributing to make a better world, living the teaching that change is synonymous with growth. Special recognition to Jakob van Wielink and his colleagues for being my guides and guardians in the Netherlands and Switzerland, making the trip possible, connecting me to people I was meant to know, and carrying me to places where I was celebrated and moved beyond words. May we all use every moment in our lives to empower each other with our differences and form a human family.

Thank you to the people who support me in my daily life—in particular, Dr. Scott McCaul and Dr. Sabina Wallach, who have never doubted my strength to endure; Gene Cook, my dance partner, who lives with utmost kindness; and Katie Anderson, my right-hand woman, who keeps me on top of everything, supports me in tackling anything, and models how to be a take-charge person. Thank you all for looking after my body, mind, and spirit, always keeping my best interests at heart, and reminding me every day that self-love is self-care.

Writing my first book was a dream come true. Publishing a second book is beyond what I ever thought possible. I couldn't have done any of it without my extraordinary team: my friend and cheerleader Wendy Walker, an inspirational role model of how to be a true survivor and live in the present; my insightful editors, Roz Lippel and Nan Graham, and their wonderful colleagues at Scribner; Jordan and Illynger Engle for the work they do sharing my message through social media; my agent, Doug Abrams, and his dream factory at Idea Architects; and my cowriter, Esmé Schwall Weigand, who takes my words and turns them into poetry.

## ACKNOWLEDGMENTS

To my daughters, Marianne and Audrey, the most powerful sisters who practice the art of agreeing to disagree, thank you for all you've taught me about choosing not to be a victim or a rescuer. And thank you for the dynamic and sensitive contributions you've made to this book, helping distill the theoretical and practical dimensions of my work. To my son, John, thank you for the courage you demonstrate every day in the way you commit yourself to others.

To the generations that come after me, and the ancestors who came before, thank you for showing me that we carry the blood of survivors. That we can always live free, never a victim of anyone or anything.

# ABOUT THE AUTHOR

An eminent psychologist and one of the few remaining Holocaust survivors old enough to remember life in the camps, Dr Edith Eger has worked with veterans, military personnel and victims of physical and mental trauma. She lives in La Jolla, California. She is the author of the award-winning *New York Times* bestseller, *The Choice*.

THE INTERNATIONAL BESTSELLER

# THE
# CHOICE

Even in hell
hope *can* flower

**EDITH EGER**

THE
AWARD-WINNING
INTERNATIONAL
BESTSELLER
BY EDITH EGER

*'I'll be forever
changed by Dr Eger's
story'*
*Oprah Winfrey*

In 1944, sixteen-year-old ballerina Edith Eger was sent to
Auschwitz. Separated from her parents on arrival, she endures
unimaginable experiences, including being made to dance for the
infamous Josef Mengele. When the camp is finally liberated,
she is pulled from a pile of bodies, barely alive.

The horrors of the Holocaust didn't break Edith. In fact, they
helped her learn to live again with a life-affirming strength and
a truly remarkable resilience.

*The Choice* is her unforgettable story. It shows that hope can flower
in the most unlikely places.

ISBN: 9781846045127

EXTRACT FROM

# The Choice

BY EDITH EGER

## I Had My Secret, and My Secret Had Me

I didn't know about the loaded gun hidden under his shirt, but the instant Captain Jason Fuller walked into my El Paso office on a summer day in 1980, my gut tightened and the back of my neck stung. War had taught me to sense danger even before I could explain why I was afraid.

Jason was tall, with the lean physique of an athlete, but his body was so rigid he appeared more wooden than human. His blue eyes looked distant, his jaw frozen, and he wouldn't—or couldn't—speak. I steered him to the white couch in my office. He sat stiffly, fists pressing into his knees. I had never met Jason and had no idea what had triggered his catatonic state. His body was close enough to touch, and his anguish practically palpable, but he was far away, lost. He did not even seem to notice my silver standard poodle, Tess, standing at attention near my desk, like a second living statue in the room.

I took a deep breath and searched for a way to begin. Sometimes I start a first session by introducing myself and sharing a little of my history and approach. Sometimes I jump right into identifying and investigating the feelings that have brought the patient to my office. With Jason, it felt critical not to overwhelm him with too much information or ask him to be too vulnerable too quickly. He was completely shut down. I had to find a way to give him the safety and permission he needed to risk showing me whatever he guarded so tightly inside. And I had to pay attention to my body's warning system without letting my sense of danger overwhelm my ability to help.

"How can I be useful to you?" I asked.

He didn't answer. He didn't even blink. He reminded me of a character in a myth or folktale who has been turned to stone. What magic spell could free him?

"Why now?" I asked. This was my secret weapon. The question I always ask my patients on a first visit. I need to know why they are motivated to change. Why today, of all days, do they want to start working with me? Why is today different from yesterday, or last week, or last year? Why is today different from tomorrow? Sometimes our pain pushes us, and sometimes our hope pulls us. Asking "Why now?" isn't just asking a question—it's asking everything.

One of his eyes briefly twitched closed. But he said nothing.

"Tell me why you're here," I invited again.

Still he said nothing.

My body tensed with a wave of uncertainty and an awareness of the tenuous and crucial crossroads where we sat: two humans face-to-face, both of us vulnerable, both of us taking a risk as we struggled to name an anguish and find its cure. Jason hadn't arrived with an official referral. It appeared that he had brought himself to my office by choice. But I knew from clinical and personal experience that even when someone chooses to heal, he or she can remain frozen for years.

Given the severity of the symptoms he exhibited, if I didn't succeed in reaching him my only alternative would be to recommend him to my colleague, the chief psychiatrist at the William Beaumont Army Medical Center, where I'd done my doctoral work. Dr. Harold Kolmer would diagnose Jason's catatonia, hospitalize him, and probably prescribe an antipsychotic drug like Haldol. I pictured Jason in a hospital gown, his eyes still glazed, his body, now so tense, racked with the muscle spasms that are often a side effect of the drugs prescribed to manage psychosis. I rely absolutely on the expertise of my psychiatrist colleagues, and I am grateful for the medications that save lives. But I don't like to jump to hospitalization if there's any chance of success with a therapeutic intervention. I feared that if I recommended Jason to be hospitalized and medicated without first exploring other options, he would trade one kind of numbness for another, frozen limbs for the involuntary movements of dyskinesia—an uncoordinated dance of repeating tics and motions, when the nervous system sends the signal for the body to move without the mind's permission. His pain, whatever its cause, might be muted by the drugs, but it wouldn't be resolved. He might feel better, or feel less—which we often mistake for feeling better—but he would not be healed.

*What now?* I wondered as the heavy minutes dragged past, as Jason sat frozen on my couch—there by choice, but still imprisoned. I had only one hour. One opportunity. Could I reach him? Could I help him to dissolve his potential for violence, which I could sense as clearly as the air conditioner's blast

239

across my skin? Could I help him see that whatever his trouble and whatever his pain, he already held the key to his own freedom? I couldn't have known then that if I failed to reach Jason on that very day, a fate far worse than a hospital room awaited him—a life in an actual prison, probably on death row. I only knew then that I had to try.

As I studied Jason, I knew that to reach him I wouldn't use the language of feelings; I would use a language more comfortable and familiar to someone in the military. I would give orders. I sensed that the only hope for unlocking him was to get the blood moving through his body.

"We're going for a walk," I said. I didn't ask. I gave the command. "Captain, we will take Tess to the park—now."

Jason looked panicked for a moment. Here was a woman, a stranger, talking in a thick Hungarian accent, telling him what to do. I could see him looking around, wondering, "How can I get out of here?" But he was a good soldier. He stood up.

"Yes, ma'am," he said. "Yes, ma'am."

I would discover soon enough the origin of Jason's trauma, and he would discover that despite our obvious differences, there was much we shared. We both knew violence. And we both knew what it was like to become frozen. I also carried a wound within me, a sorrow so deep that for many years I hadn't been able to speak of it at all, to anyone.

My past still haunted me: an anxious, dizzy feeling every time I heard sirens, or heavy footsteps, or shouting men. This, I had learned, is trauma: a nearly constant feeling in my gut that something is wrong, or that something terrible is about to happen, the automatic fear responses in my body telling me to run away, to take cover, to hide myself from the danger that is everywhere. My trauma can still rise up out of mundane encounters. A sudden sight, a particular smell, can transport me back to the past. The day I met Captain Fuller, more than thirty years had passed since I'd been liberated from the concentration camps of the Holocaust. Today, more than seventy years have passed. What happened can never be forgotten and can never be changed. But over time I learned that I can choose how to respond to the past. I can be miserable, or I can be hopeful—I can be depressed, or I can be happy. We always have that choice, that opportunity for control. *I'm here, this is now*, I have learned to tell myself, over and over, until the panicky feeling begins to ease.

Conventional wisdom says that if something bothers you or causes you anxiety, then just don't look at it. Don't dwell on it. Don't go there. So we run from past traumas and hardships or from current discomfort or conflict. For much of my adulthood I had thought my survival in the present depended on keeping the past and its darkness locked away. In my early immigrant years in Baltimore in the 1950s, I didn't even know how to pronounce Auschwitz in English. Not that I would have wanted to tell you I was there even if I could have. I didn't want anyone's pity. I didn't want anyone to know.

I just wanted to be a Yankee doodle dandy. To speak English without an accent. To hide from the past. In my yearning to belong, in my fear of being swallowed up by the past, I worked very hard to keep my pain hidden. I hadn't yet discovered that my silence and my desire for acceptance, both founded in fear, were ways of running away from myself—that in choosing not to face the past and myself directly, decades after my literal imprisonment had ended, I was still choosing not to be free. I had my secret, and my secret had me.

The catatonic Army captain sitting immobile on my couch reminded me of what I had eventually discovered: that when we force our truths and stories into hiding, secrets can become their own trauma, their own prison. Far from diminishing pain, whatever we deny ourselves the opportunity to accept becomes as inescapable as brick walls and steel bars. When we don't allow ourselves to grieve our losses, wounds, and disappointments, we are doomed to keep reliving them.

Freedom lies in learning to embrace what happened. Freedom means we muster the courage to dismantle the prison, brick by brick.

\* \* \*

Bad things, I am afraid, happen to everyone. This we can't change. If you look at your birth certificate, does it say life will be easy? It does not. But so many of us remain stuck in a trauma or grief, unable to experience our lives fully. This we can change.

At Kennedy International Airport recently, waiting for my flight home to San Diego, I sat and studied the faces of every passing stranger. What I saw deeply moved me. I saw boredom, fury, tension, worry, confusion, discouragement, disappointment, sadness, and, most troubling of all, emptiness. It made me very sad to see so little joy and laughter. Even the dullest moments of our lives are opportunities to experience hope, buoyancy, happiness. Mundane life is life too. As is painful life, and stressful life. Why do we so often struggle to feel alive, or distance ourselves from feeling life fully? Why is it such a challenge to bring life to life?

If you asked me for the most common diagnosis among the people I treat, I wouldn't say depression or post-traumatic stress disorder, although these conditions are all too common among those I've known, loved, and guided to freedom. No, I would say hunger. We are hungry. We are hungry for approval, attention, affection. We are hungry for the freedom to embrace life and to really know and be ourselves.

My own search for freedom and my years of experience as a licensed clinical psychologist have taught me that suffering is universal. But victimhood is optional. There is a difference between victimization and victimhood. We are all likely to be victimized in some way in the course of our lives. At some point we will suffer some kind of affliction or calamity or abuse, caused by circumstances or people or institutions over which we have little or no control. This is life. And this is victimization. It comes from the outside. It's the neighborhood bully, the boss who rages, the spouse who hits, the lover who cheats, the discriminatory law, the accident that lands you in the hospital.

In contrast, victimhood comes from the inside. No one can make you a victim but you. We become victims not because of what happens to us but when we choose to hold on to our victimization. We develop a victim's mind—a way of thinking and being that is rigid, blaming, pessimistic, stuck in the past, unforgiving, punitive, and without healthy limits or boundaries. We become our own jailors when we choose the confines of the victim's mind.

I want to make one thing very clear. When I talk about victims and survivors, I am not blaming victims—so many of whom never had a chance. I could never blame those who were sent right to the gas chambers or who died in their cot, or even those who ran into the electric barbed wire fence. I grieve for all people everywhere who are sentenced to violence and destruction. I live to guide others to a position of empowerment in the face of all of life's hardships.

I also want to say that there is no hierarchy of suffering. There's nothing that makes my pain worse or better than yours, no graph on which we can plot the relative importance of one sorrow versus another. People say to me, "Things in my life are pretty hard right now, but I have no right to complain—it's not *Auschwitz*." This kind of comparison can lead us to minimize or diminish our own suffering. Being a survivor, being a "thriver" requires absolute acceptance of what was and what is. If we discount our pain, or punish ourselves for feeling lost or isolated or scared about the challenges in our lives, however insignificant these challenges may seem to someone else, then we're still choosing to be victims. We're not seeing our choices. We're judging ourselves. I don't want you to hear my story and say, "My own suffering is less significant." I want you to hear my story and say, "If she can do it, then so can I!"

One morning I saw two patients back to back, both mothers in their forties. The first woman had a daughter who was dying of hemophilia. She spent most of her visit crying, asking how God could take her child's life. I hurt so much for this woman— she was absolutely devoted to her daughter's care, and devastated by her impending loss. She was angry, she was grieving, and she wasn't at all sure that she could survive the hurt.

My next patient had just come from the country club, not the hospital. She, too, spent much of the hour crying. She was upset because her new Cadillac had just been delivered, and it was the wrong shade of yellow. On the surface, her problem seemed petty, especially compared to my previous patient's anguish over her dying child. But I knew enough about her to understand that her tears of disappointment over the color of her car were really tears of disappointment over the bigger things in her life that hadn't worked out the way she had hoped—a lonely marriage, a son who had been kicked out of yet another school, the aspirations for a career she had abandoned in order to be more available for her husband and child. Often, the little upsets in our lives are emblematic of the larger losses; the seemingly insignificant worries are representative of greater pain.

I realized that day how much my two patients, who appeared so different, had in common—with each other and with all people everywhere. Both women were responding to a situation they couldn't control in which their expectations had been upended. Both were struggling and hurting because something was not what they wanted or expected it to be; they were trying to reconcile what was with what ought to have been. Each woman's pain was real. Each woman was caught up in the human drama—that we find ourselves in situations we didn't see coming and that we don't feel prepared to handle. Both women deserved my compassion. Both had the potential to heal. Both women, like all of us, had choices in attitude and action that could move them from victim to survivor even if the circumstances they were dealing with didn't change. Survivors don't have time to ask, "Why me?" For survivors, the only relevant question is, "What now?"

Whether you're in the dawn or noon or late evening of your life, whether you've seen deep suffering or are only just beginning to encounter struggle, whether you're falling in love for the first time or losing your life partner to old age, whether you're healing from a life-altering event or in search of some little adjustments that could bring more joy to your life, I would love to help you discover how to escape the concentration camp of your own mind and become the person you were meant to be. I would love to help you experience freedom from the past, freedom from failures and fears, freedom from anger and mistakes, freedom from regret and unresolved grief—and the freedom to enjoy the full, rich feast of life. We cannot choose to have a life free of hurt. But we can choose to be free, to escape the past, no matter what befalls us, and to embrace the possible. I invite you to make the choice to be free.

Like the challah my mother used to make for our Friday night meal, this book has three strands: my story of survival, my story of healing myself, and the stories of the precious people I've had the privilege of guiding to freedom. I've conveyed my experience as I can best remember it. The stories about patients accurately reflect the core of their experiences, but I have changed all names and identifying details and in some instances created composites from patients working through similar challenges. What follows is the story of the choices, big and small, that can lead us from trauma to triumph, from darkness to light, from imprisonment to freedom.